TO GIVE
AND GIVE AGAIN

TO GIVE
AND
GIVE AGAIN

A Christian Imperative for Generosity

DONALD W. HINZE

THE PILGRIM PRESS
NEW YORK

Biblical quotations, unless otherwise noted, are from the Revised Standard Version of the Bible, copyright 1946, 1952, © 1971, 1973 by the Division of Christian Education of the National Council of the Churches of Christ in the U.S.A., and are used by permission.

Elise Maclay, "Worldly Goods," from *Green Winter.* Copyright © 1977, 1990 by Elise Maclay. Reprinted by arrangement with Henry Holt and Company, Inc.

Library of Congress Cataloging-in-Publication Data

Hinze, Donald W.
To give and give again : a Christian imperative for generosity / Donald W. Hinze.
    p.   cm.
Includes bibliographical references.
ISBN 0-8298-0830-2
1. Christian giving. 2. Stewardship, Christian. 3. Generosity.
I. Title.
BV772.H516   1990
248'.6—dc20   89-78180
                                                  CIP

The Pilgrim Press, 475 Riverside Drive, New York, NY 10115

CONTENTS

INTRODUCTION

The third stanza of Harry Emerson Fosdick's great hymn of 1930, "God of Grace and God of Glory," petitioned God: "Shame our wonton, selfish gladness, Rich in things and poor in soul. Grant us wisdom, Grant us courage, Lest we miss thy kingdom's goal." Writing during the Great Depression, Fosdick could not have imagined the richness in things that would overflood Americans in the latter half of this century. Our unprecedented wealth and prosperity, unchecked and ill-managed, has led us to a poverty of soul. We are becoming the incarnate answer to the eternal question in Luke 9:25, "For what does it profit a man if he gains the whole world and loses or forfeits himself?" Only God's gift of grace combined with our own wisdom and courage will reset our course toward the kingdom's goal of the care and stewardship of all life.

In this volume I redefine and discuss what is, at the same time, America's and the First World's blessing and curse. So fervent is our quest for material fortune that it has taken on religious proportions. In the decades since World War II, Americans, including those in the mainline denominations, have seen new visions and dreamed new

INTRODUCTION

The third stanza of Harry Emerson Fosdick's great hymn of 1930, "God of Grace and God of Glory," petitioned God: "Shame our wonton, selfish gladness, Rich in things and poor in soul. Grant us wisdom, Grant us courage, Lest we miss thy kingdom's goal." Writing during the Great Depression, Fosdick could not have imagined the richness in things that would overflood Americans in the latter half of this century. Our unprecedented wealth and prosperity, unchecked and ill-managed, has led us to a poverty of soul. We are becoming the incarnate answer to the eternal question in Luke 9:25, "For what does it profit a man if he gains the whole world and loses or forfeits himself?" Only God's gift of grace combined with our own wisdom and courage will reset our course toward the kingdom's goal of the care and stewardship of all life.

In this volume I redefine and discuss what is, at the same time, America's and the First World's blessing and curse. So fervent is our quest for material fortune that it has taken on religious proportions. In the decades since World War II, Americans, including those in the mainline denominations, have seen new visions and dreamed new dreams of success and material gain. So beguiling is this American dream that it has superseded the vision of faith and morality that had been the hallmark of American Christians. As in imperial Rome, traditional religious faith has become a matter of observance rather than devotion. As churches decline in influence, mammon becomes the new object of worship and service.

Can our course be changed? If America's gift is the ability to enterprise and to attain great profit, can the gift be reconceived as God given? Can its fruits be stewarded for the benefit of all humankind? Few in biblical literature or world history have been able successfully to come to terms with wealth and power. The gospel is replete with lessons about rich fools, would-be followers possessed by wealth, and rich persons oblivious to the poor and hungry at their gates. Conversion to the ethic of stewardship is our only hope. It is America's and the American churches' spiritual burden; just as others may be claimed by God at their own points of strength in other circumstances, Americans, blessed with the goods of this world, are claimed by faith at the place of their treasure. We are given a singular opportunity to revision the kingdom's goal.

Central to this position is my belief that as humans we live, move, and have our being as a result of God's graceful action in the world. As I view life and creation from the biblical perspective the picture I see is of an endlessly giving God involved in every aspect of our understanding of God's action, from the Old Testament recital of the gift of creation and life, to Jesus who gives himself in total abandon, stripping himself of every advantage, and finally to the Spirit who is known as the bearer of gifts. Made after God's own likeness, humans are called to be imitators of God, givers and stewards of all things in furthering the work of creation. It is the unmistakable way to meaning and purpose in human life.

I contend that generosity with gifts is the way to spiritual maturity. Sacred and secular history and literature are replete with examples of the crippling effects of gifts hoarded and unshared. Personally, socially, and internationally, people are not naturally disposed to giving. Yet, the life we all prize, filled with joy and spiritual depth, is closely tied to giving generously and with thankful hearts. Wherever our treasure is, known by the presence of our heart, this is where we must generously share and steward our gift. The best interests of one's own self are always best served through the generous giving of the self and its gifts. Do we give because of our faith commitment? Or can grateful giving lead us to new faith commitment? Perhaps the relationship is reciprocal.

Christian faith rests clearly on the conviction that we are created, sustained, and saved by God's grace alone. Yet in the living of our brief moments of time we are called to good works (Eph. 2:10) by the stewardship of all that we have and are. In worship we give thanks for all of the gifts of life undeservedly received, for the unmerited forgiveness received; at the same time we bring a gift, a response which we call an offering. It is always so in the Judeo-Christian heritage: thanks for gifts and a corresponding gift; receiving and giving before Creator Giver and creature giver. Bringing our gifts before God is a sacramental moment in the context of all life.

In this volume I look at the malaise of the American Christian church near the close of this century (we could very well include churches of the Western world). Are we like Israel in exile, bound in captivity to goods and possessions? Theologian Bruce Birch, of Wesley Theological Seminary, points out that the people of Israel could not sing in exile (Psalm 137); the song would not come any longer. Perhaps this is why we do not sing well in our churches today. Is penurious giving to the church a symptom? Or does the very disease of consumerism and materialism so captivate us that generosity and stewardship are held in bondage? The gospels are clear about the peril possessions pose to spiritual health. Instructive though discomforting for today's church is the fact that the most distinguishing mark of the first post-Pentecost Christian church (Acts 1—5) was that it was built around the adherents' relationship to their possessions.

The failures of stewardship take many forms: greed, mismanagement, inequity and the abuse of our gifts are a few. Humans were charged with "dominion" over the creation given to them. We have mistaken dominion to mean conquest and perverted use rather than stewardship. Instead of caretaking creation and its gifts we have exploited and raped them.

For stewardship to have a chance it must begin with the serious question, What do I owe to life for the freely received gift of life and its accompanying benefits? The conversion to stewardship begins with the rejection of the idea that we have personally earned, deserved, acquired or won anything we possess. Everything is a gift! In his call to the people of Israel to remember the source of their existence and their gifts, Moses warned, "Beware, lest you say in your heart, 'My power and the might of my hand have gotten me this wealth.' You shall remember the Lord your God, for it is he who gives you power to get wealth" (Deut. 8:17–18). Moses further admonished them not to forget that if they go after other gods (of profit and possessions) they will surely perish. Stewardship begins with the recognition that all of life is interdependent, that we have received many gifts from others and from God, and that a grateful generous response is our task and calling.

What should be the nature and extent of the gift we give? The reply to this question is central to the three great monotheistic religious traditions. The Old Testament of

TO GIVE
AND GIVE AGAIN

1.

THE RELIGION
OF PROFITS
AND POSSESSIONS

> It is preoccupation with possessions, more than anything else,
> that prevents persons from living freely and nobly.
> —Bertrand Russell, *Principles of Social Reconstruction* (1916)

A serious condition exists today in America and the First World, a condition that drains our strength, divides our minds, scrambles our emotions and blocks our spiritual centers. The condition is overabundance, and the accompanying endless hunger for more. Its effect upon Christians, and particularly the American church, has been devastating. Our preoccupation with getting and spending is destroying our awareness of God, who is within us.

Much has been observed and written recently about the decline of mainline American Protestantism since the 1960s. Once the blossoming of the sixteenth-century Reformation heritage, the denominations have been on a slippery slope in the last third of this century.[1] Many arguments and theories have been advanced as reasons for

1

the decline. One theory blames the liberal stances the denominations have taken on political and social issues. A retreat from former zeal in the world missionary field is another reason; disregard for media power in the resources of radio and television has also been cited as a factor. Feeble efforts in evangelism for church growth indicate an obvious area of neglect among the mainline Protestant church bodies which now represent less than 25 percent of all American Christians.

I believe that at the root of the downward curve is the failure in Christian stewardship relative to personal and institutional wealth. Mainline Protestantism has traditionally and historically been at the center of creative theological ferment, in the forefront of American higher education, predominant in the Protestant world missionary enterprise and the focal point of the ecumenical movement of the one church for the whole world. Further it was the bellwether for American cultural, moral and religious values. The great social crusades of this nation were spearheaded by mainline churches: anti-slavery, women's rights, prohibition, anti-war movements. But then as we moved into the 1960s, Martin Luther King, Jr., admonished us that American churches were not the headlight of the civil rights movement but the taillight. The gathering of wealth and power, rather than social issues, was becoming a more important concern to the churches.

Since World War II the members of these American denominations have benefited in the accumulation of wealth and power. They are the middle- and upper-class achievers of goods and property. Increasingly they dominated the government of the United States, holding a majority of seats in both houses of Congress, as well as the office of the president. When Dwight D. Eisenhower became a professing Presbyterian in the early 1950s, mainline churches were the standard-bearers of America's faith.

They were strong and influential, their members growing in prosperity. Earlier, the senior Rockefeller, a mainline Baptist, built the eminent Riverside Church in New York City as the pulpit for Harry Emerson Fosdick, a mainline "superstar."

Have American mainline Protestants become possessors of comparative wealth and power? The current sprinkling of unexpected major financial bequests from aging members to their local congregations would indicate so. As monied and aging members approach the twenty-first century, the sprinkling could become a major shower. Will congregations be able to steward their unexpected wealth? Or will they clutch it and hoard its earnings as culture has taught us so well? In an irony of the faith, countless congregations have been undone by windfall riches.

As spiritual energies have been diverted to the pursuit of wealth, the seductive sirens of goods and gain gradually but relentlessly began to drown out the songs, prayers and preachings of the faith. The God of Abraham, Isaac and Jacob, of Christ and the apostles was superseded by the gods of wealth and consumerism. The Judeo-Christian traditions, though proclaimed steadfastly in name, have become subservient to the religion of profits and possessions. With the post-war gift of material opportunity and gain, many people, including mainline communicants, came under the spell of the unprecedented accumulation of money and property. The allure was like the pull of gravity. The desire for things became a religious quest. Stewardship was buried and forgotten and still awaits resurrection.

In the mainline churches' slow downward spiral, the personal commitment to Judeo-Christian values has been displaced by a commitment to monetary values, and the biblical stewardship of life by the pursuit of material well-being. It could not be otherwise; the timeless values of the eternal can receive only lip service when the past is but dimly remembered. This is the condition of the mainline churches and their members as we enter the 1990s. The members are prosperous and comfortable; their churches, as low priorities, are in decline. We are reminded of the prosperous farmer who had a voracious appetite for more land. When asked about this, he stated, "I really don't want that much. I only want the land next to mine." Where is the end of the lust for more?

In our hearts, we all know that the American Dream is not "liberty and justice for all," nor is it the common good of all. Rather it is the chance personally to "strike it rich" by whatever means. One of our nation's most prestigious financial publications, *The Wall Street Journal*, has as its advertising subtitle "The Daily Diary of the American Dream." Such dreams are not limited to the greedy and avaricious few but are at the heart of the quest for meaning many have embarked upon. Common are the overcommitment to work for more money or the excitement over a hot tip on the stock market. One has only to view the hysteria of hitting it big on a television game show or in the state lottery, or the dream of a chance inheritance from a wealthy relative. Winners of millions of dollars in state-sponsored lotteries rate front page newspaper coverage again and again. Non-resident gamblers flock into states with multi-million dollar jackpots in the hope of winning the big one even against fourteen million-to-one odds. Who does not yearn for the possibility of such windfalls?

Sociological studies indicate that people are using money and possessions to fill the vacuum left by the weakening of institutions like community, religion, school and, especially, family. These institutions have traditionally helped give life meaning and security, which a luxury car or diamond necklace just cannot do.

Lord Acton's famous maxim, "Power tends to corrupt; absolute power corrupts absolutely," has overshadowed another profound remark he made: "Every institution tends to perish by an excess of its own basic principle." The excesses of the capitalist system turn in on themselves and become the cause of their own demise. Today we see just the tip of the iceberg in deals, plots, leveraged buyouts, takeovers and acquisitions. Note the "insider trading" scams of Dennis Levine, Ivan Boesky and others, the fraudulent dealing of "junk bond king" Michael Milken and his respected company Drexel Burnham Lambert. Milken regularly earned for himself a million dollars daily before lunch. In the public sphere was the HUD (Housing and Urban Development) scandal of fraud and greed in which former federal government officials and private citizens profited personally by siphoning billions of taxpayer dollars intended for the poor and homeless. All of this because there is so much money to be had out there.

While many such practices are criminal and fraught with corruption, there is a vast gray area of financial wheeling and dealing that is manipulative and opportunistic though technically legal. "Symbolic analysis," for example, is a term that economist Robert Reich uses to describe work that includes the manipulation of information for profit: investment banking, law and research science—all from the computer terminal. Symbolic analysis involves dealing on the telephone, watching the Quotron screen for latebreaking financial news, pressing the computer keys. It is one way to make big money these days.

Most Americans do not have access to or the ability to capitalize on this huge money market, but the desire is there, and as long as the method is not illegal, the end justifies the means. Americans feel that they are entitled to be well-off. Indeed, in every year since 1945 most of us, especially the often-privileged members of mainline churches, have been worth more financially than we were the year before.

In 1986 Ivan P. Boesky, one of the four hundred wealthiest persons in the world and recently fined a hundred million dollars and imprisoned for his fraudulent mega-million gains, became something of a yuppie folk hero when he addressed University of California–Berkeley Business School graduates and extolled greed as good. Something is wrong when desire turns to greed, and greed and acquisition are seen as the essence of the evolutionary spirit of economics. America has a voracious appetite for material gain and goods and continues to devise ever-higher standards of living and to demand greater quantities of consumer goods. Greed, even on the small scale practiced by average Americans, generates enormous destructive powers.

Meanwhile, the ethics of business have so pained John Shad, the outgoing chairman of the Securities and Exchange Commission, which monitors securities and financial markets, that he has personally given Harvard University $30 million to endow a Chair of ethics. Could our nation's founding fathers or our mainline ancestors ever have imagined that the largest single grant ever to Harvard would be to train business people in ethics and honesty?

Learning about acquisition begins early. During a day of relaxation following a conference we joined many other guests around the pool for a few moments in the sun. A recreation director appeared and invited all the children under age ten to a water activity. All of you jump in the pool at waist depth was the instruction. When I blow the whistle I'll throw in these pennies, and the one who can get the most will get a special reward. As the mad scramble began, there were soon hassles over territorial rights. A mother from Britain looked over and said, "The first lesson in greed." It was, and clearly the child with thirty pennies was more resourceful than the one with eighteen, and received a dollar bill as a bonus. You've got to grab and go for it.

How important is money and wealth? Note the anguish and grief over the occasion of "Black Monday," the stock market tumble, October 19, 1987. The day has been given a name in history, and is one of those days every American remembers, such as December 7, 1941 or the day when President Kennedy was assassinated. It was a critical moment for the wealthy and the prosperous. A financial services manager in California said he took the day in stride: "I slept like a baby that night. Every hour I woke up and cried." Another said, "I knew the stock market was in trouble when I called my broker and got Dial-a-Prayer." It was an American style catastrophe of cosmic and religious proportions.

Does anyone question that for First World people of privilege, that is, for most Americans, the sacred mission has become the acquisition of money and the accumulation of assets? Private profit is a goal more cherished than public good. The quest for money and possessions is as fervent, personal and private as a religious endeavor. Harry Golden said, "People never discuss their salaries publicly, or their income, or patrimony. People make a successful effort never to discuss money in front of friends or relatives, because money in our society is the ultimate reality and to discuss it is to reveal one's self."[2] It is one's holy of holies. Money and material things become the graven images of our idolatry.

My purpose here is not to debate or analyze world economic theories; church bodies have recently produced extensive and important documents on the national and world economies relative to the Christian faith.[3] It is sufficient here to say that Americans, including those in mainline churches, and others in the First World enjoy an unprecedented standard of living and that the unending pursuit of this expanding goal has become for many a matter of religious passion. I will discuss the ways in which this bears on typical mainline churches in later chapters.

WIDENING GAPS AND SPIRITUAL POVERTY

The quest for profit and things has consequences which are devastating and far-reaching. Two areas in particular demand our attention. The first is the growing disparity in America and the Third World between the rich and the poor. The second is the personal psycho-spiritual poverty that afflicts those who have become mesmerized by the profits/possessions cult.

THE *HAVES* VS THE *HAVE NOTS:* ECONOMIC POVERTY

One of the dangerous consequences of Western prosperity is the gap between the rich and the poor, a gap growing at the expense of the poor. This has become one of the most tragic and urgent problems of our day. We all know the ugly facts of the economic disparity among the peoples of earth: that developing nations are less the victims of underdevelopment than they are the victims of overexploitation by the wealthy and powerful; that the rich and comfortable are the passive oppressors of the poor. Having privilege and at the same time withholding from the poor is a failure of stewardship and an offense to the God of Life.

Imagine the world's billions of people reduced to a community of one thousand. Of that thousand, sixty are Americans (nearly half of them members of mainline denominations, including Roman Catholics); the other 940 represent the rest of the world. The sixty Americans have a life expectancy of seventy-four years, the other 940 about forty years. The sixty Americans have one-half of the income of the whole town and fifteen times as many possessions per person as all the rest. The lowest income group of the sixty would be far better off than the average of the rest. The vast majority of the 940 are uneducated, poor, hungry and sick. How poignant is the pain of our brothers and sisters who are left poor, unemployed, homeless and living on the edge of the abyss. A friend of mine recently saw a political poster in El Salvador that quoted Pope John Paul II: "The privileges of the few are an affront to the misery of the many."

It is impossible to square this economic disparity and these conditions with the Christian faith. The cries of the prophets ring in our ears again: "But let justice roll down like waters, and righteousness like an ever-flowing stream" (Amos 5:24); "And what does the Lord require of you but to do justice, and to love mercy, and to walk humbly with your God" (Micah 6:8). And again, there are the disturbing themes that dominate much of the gospel in parables and story, stewardship themes about the privileged and prosperous and how they live relative to their goods and the poverty of the dispossessed. Matthew 19:16–22 tells of Jesus and the rich young man who kept the commandments. Yet Jesus discerned that his obsession with wealth blocked his religious quest. He was told to sell all that he had and give it to the poor and then he would be spiritually conditioned. But his commitment to money and goods was too great; they were held deeply in his heart and he could not dislodge them. His possessions were his "holy of holies."

Luke 12:16–21 tells of the rich farmer who was so engrossed in his wealth and barns that he forgot his duties toward God and others. Jesus did not even call him a sinner for his failure of stewardship, just a "fool."

Most discomforting of all for us is Jesus' parable about Lazarus, a beggar, wasted and sick, lying at the gate of the rich man who wore purple and fine linen and feasted sumptuously every day, ignoring Lazarus and his need (Luke 16:19–31). This haunting parable inspired Albert Schweitzer to surrender fame and fortune and pursue his medical mission in Africa. He saw Europe as the rich and gifted man and dark Africa as Lazarus lying at its feet.

These are examples of a disturbing gospel, but, as Douglas John Hall says, "An inoffensive gospel is a contradiction in terms."[4]

While imperfect humans cannot create a perfect eco-society, our stewardship mandate does not absolve individuals or the church from redressing economic and social ills. Their unwillingness to come to terms with stewarding their own wealth has undermined the health of mainline churches and their individual members. It will require a radical conversion to move from the idolatry of wealth to a faithful stewarding of personal and community resources. The God of Life looked at creation and found it good and adequate for all. We can, in imitation, use the resources offered us in farm and factory to create a community in which no one need starve or go naked or unhoused.

As world economic disparity increases, it is small wonder that the overexploited Third World nations turn to revolution. To quote Blaise Pascal, "Where we do not fortify justice, we justify force." Naturally, Third World upheaval becomes discomforting to the minority rich, who see the majority poor growing in numbers, worsening in condition, and threatening to the minority status quo. Centuries ago, Aristotle observed that "poverty is the parent of revolution and crime." The West's failed stewardship practices toward the world have laid the groundwork for political and economic revolution. We have hated and feared communism more than we have hated and feared injustice. Engrossed by the gods of wealth and power, ignoring the divine call to stewardship, the churches and the society in which they are set turn their backs on the suffering world and then are haunted by fear of the consequences. To these unresponsive but powerful and entrenched groups I repeat a phrase from Howard Thurman, "Always, life is against that which has arrived; life is on the side of that which is coming." Is there still time for repentance and for hardened hearts to be changed? As the haves of the world withhold and deny their abundant resources to those who have not, the neglect is more than oversight, it is sin in the judgment of the Eternal. Repent indeed! Morality clearly dictates that stealing or "taking from" is a crime. The commandment orders us not to steal. But, according to Truman B. Douglass, "In our complex and interdependent world, there is no moral distinction between 'taking from' and 'keeping from.' Both are forms of violence—of the suppression of another's life for the advantage of your own."[5]

The church's responsibility is to become unchained from the fetters of personal and corporate wealth, great profits and holdings. Unleashing the potential of material gains and reserves on behalf of the numberless majority of the excluded, exploited and impoverished billions is a response to the call to stewardship. Roman Catholic Bishop Fulton J. Sheen once made a strong case for the haves of the world to view the have-nots as an opportunity for grace. How do the needs of the poor speak to us? He wrote,

> To de-egotize ourselves that we may have less need of psychoanalytic couches, to acknowledge God's blessing, to share our wealth, to prove ourselves trustees (stewards) of His gifts, to make up for our failings and our sins, to have grace in our hearts and the blessing of God in our whole being, to see Christ hidden in the Indian, the Moslem, the Asian, the Af-

rican: "I was hungry and you gave me to eat." Without us, they would lack for bread for the body, but without them we would lack the milk of human kindness and the joy of service. Take us out of the world and the material advantages would be lost; take them out of the world and spiritual advantages would be lost.[6]

As Mother Teresa says, "We all have so much to give, to share, to contribute wherever we find ourselves to be living."[7] This release would not even require the voluntary poverty of Mother Teresa's Sisters of Charity, but voluntary sharing in generous portions, an identification with the poor, which can relieve our own poverty of spirit and present the possibility of a new freedom from the tyranny of possessions.

What are the alternatives before us in the presence of the privileged few and the deprived billions? In *The Eternal Now,* Paul Tillich, a great personal mentor, speaks on "The Riddle of Inequality":

There is an ultimate unity of all beings, rooted in the divine life from which they emerge and to which they return. All beings, nonhuman as well as human, participate in it. And therefore they all participate in each other. And we participate in each other's having and in each other's not having. When we become aware of this unity of all beings, something happens to us. The fact that others do not have changes the character of our having: it undercuts our security and drives us beyond ourselves to understand, to give, to share, to help. The fact that others fall into sin, crime and misery alters the character of the grace that is given us: it makes us recognize our own hidden guilt; it shows us that those who suffer for their sin and crime suffer also for us, for we are guilty of their guilt and ought to suffer as they suffer. Our becoming aware of the fact that others who could have developed into full human beings did not, changes our state of full humanity. Their early death, their early or late disintegration, brings to our own personal life and health a continuous risk, a dying that is not yet death, a disintegration that is not yet destruction. In every death we encounter, something of us dies, and in every disease, something of us tends toward disintegration. Can we live with this answer? We can to the degree to which we are liberated from seclusion in ourselves.[8]

SPIRITUAL POVERTY

A second peril that accompanies prosperity is the undermining destruction of one's own psycho-spiritual orientation. As Jesus warned in the Sermon on the Mount: "No one can serve two masters. . . . You cannot serve God and mammon [riches]" (Matt. 6:24). This peril involves irreconcilable differences. Jesus also recognized this conflict in the rich young man in Luke 16:19–31 who was trying to be religious and pursue wealth at the same time. It is also reflected in the question, "What does it profit a person to gain the whole world and lose their soul?" (Luke 9:25). We cannot have both, though we have tried to do just that in our churches and our lives. The combination has resulted in our "religious" passion for wealth.

In creation's intent, it would appear that people were made for others, for community and sharing. The religious and virtuous life is found in goodwill and right relations with others, in treating all as members of each other. It is difficult, however, to harmonize this style of religious understanding with a life that is preoccupied with wealth and possessions. The Victorian historian and social critic Thomas Carlyle spoke to the point: "Adversity is sometimes hard upon a man; but for one man who can stand prosperity, there are a hundred that will stand adversity." The demands of wealth and privilege are so consuming and alluring that they absorb all attention and block the way to spiritual awareness. "Things" become sacred and important and have precedence over God and people. My experience in the mainline church indicates that most people try to have both spirituality and wealth; they lose or fool themselves in the process.

In his existentialist diary, *Having and Being*, Gabriel Marcel argues, "The more I treat my own ideas, or my stables or greenhouse, as something belonging to me, the more surely will these possessions, by their very inertia, exercise a tyrannical power over me. Acquiring and keeping are exhausting, all-consuming pursuits." Marcel examines, "the nature of the relative dependency of being and having: our possessions swallow us up. The self becomes incorporated in the thing possessed. To possess is almost inevitably to be possessed. Things possessed get in the way." The purpose of having is to supply the needs of our incompleteness. We are hungry and we need to have food. When the hunger is satisfied through our having (food), the satisfaction even assured for many meals and nourishment beyond the present, the excess then becomes a matter of retaining and stockpiling. At this point, the asset of having begins to become the liability of keeping and withholding. "I wonder," Marcel writes, "if we could not define the whole spiritual life as the sum of activities by which we try to reduce in ourselves the part played by non-disposability. Death is the flat denial of nondisposability."[9]

Stewardship invites us to the reality of disposability and to the tasks of practicing dispossession. Think about our anticipation of death. Would the specter of death be as disturbing if we could begin the practice of relinquishing something of ourselves daily? If we have the opportunity to be aware of our final moments of life, perhaps we could then let go in glad and reckless abandon. We could see death not as taking life from us but as something to which we *give* our lives in joyous liberation.

In a wonderful poem entitled "Green Winter, A Celebration of Old Age," Elise Maclay portrays one relationship to "Worldly Goods":

> I'm giving away my things
> And it turns out to be

As much of an occupation
And as much fun
As collecting them was.
I browse among my friends the way
I used to browse in shops.
I try to decide who should have the cameo
I wore as a bride, who would like
My Chinese vase. I go through closets and drawers
And am amazed at what I find.
So many objects. I am ashamed
To have so much when so many have so little.
Worse still, there are a lot of things I hardly ever use.
This handsome fish poacher, for example.
Hammered copper. It came from France.
I used it once or twice. We thought a meal had to be
Meat and potatoes. The kids know better.
My daughter-in-law, Jill, eats only vegetables and fish.
She says it saves grain for the hungry and is a less
    aggressive way
To live. Bless her heart, she is a gentle child,
She'll love this poacher, and my silver napkin rings
(She won't use paper napkins—says she wants no tree
To die to wipe her mouth). It takes forever,
Sorting things, I stop to think about where and when
And I find myself thinking, I may have use for this
    again.
Nonsense. I don't bake angel food cakes anymore,
Give the pan away. Funny, I thought I'd feel a sense of
    loss
With fewer of my things around.
I don't.
I feel exhilarated, free.
Is this why You told the rich man to sell his goods?
I think now your command
Was meant to help the rich man more.[10]

Can we of the church see Christian worship as stewardship in the sense in which Marcel speaks of worship—"an act of simultaneously throwing oneself open and offering oneself up"? For, he says, "Pure religion constitutes a realm over which we can obtain no hold [no possession] at all. To pure religion we come simply to give ourselves up."[11] This is an approach to the faith that begins as stewardship, as measuring and accounting our gifts, including life itself, and then setting about the task of practicing release and dispossession. This, then, is beginning to learn the lesson that the rich, young man who came to Jesus could not accept; and it is the way to serve one "master," not mammon, but God, with singleness of heart. It finally will bring wholeness to our splintered and divided selves.

The saving act of God's grace notwithstanding, does a declining church have a chance to be useful as an instrument of God's mission and purpose? Can we be turned away from our avaricious pursuits? We can begin by putting our citadels of power—our earthly gifts—personal and institutional, under the scrutiny of stewardship, at the disposal of the Creator's purpose.

2.

THE STEWARDING OF OUR ABUNDANCE

> The love of Jesus is both avid and generous.
> All that he is and all that he has, he gives.
> All that we are and all that we have, he takes.
> —Jan Van Ruysbroeck (1293–1381)

Can the Judeo-Christian stewardship ethic prevail as the measure of human behavior in the western world when the hunger for wealth and possessions is the driving force behind the human quest? This question leads me to the conclusion that Judeo-Christian teaching is an anachronism in those situations in which goods and money are either sacrosanct or the gauge of meaning and personal human worth. Yet, it is precisely in those situations in which the ethic of stewardship is most foreign and unwelcome that its transforming power is most urgently required. Stewardship is unknown where one basks in prosperity while another languishes in want.

THE DUALITY OF STEWARDSHIP

Stewardship is what we do with what creation gives to us. It is the acquisition, accumulation and management of gifts. But it is more: stewardship is the sharing, giving and release of resources. It invites us to practice generosity with thankful hearts. Where we know only gathering and keeping, it teaches us that we are out of step with creation, that creation is harmonized by the cyclic rhythm of receiving and giving, the alternation of having and yielding.

Wealth and comfort are not readily compatible with spiritual vitality unless they are coupled with strong impulses for generosity, service and uncommon sharing. In our time and place of superabundance, when we know the price of everything but the value of little, the relationship of people and communities to their goods and possessions is central to any faith expression. Having much but giving little is an offense to the pursuit and practice of Christianity, especially in the face of the coexistent presence of enormous wealth and gross poverty in our own country and around the world. The Spirit yearns for those who have to respond to those who have not. In a Hasidic story, the wife of the Rabbi of Roptchitz says to him, "Your prayer was lengthy today. Have you succeeded in bringing it about that the rich should be more generous in their gifts to the poor?" The Rabbi replies, "Half of my prayer I have accomplished. The poor are willing to accept them." The human spirit suffers in the disparities between rich and poor.

The apostle Paul wrote, "If I speak in the tongues of men and of angels, but have not love [*caritas*, charity or love in action], I am a noisy gong or a clanging cymbal" (1 Cor. 13:1). And the poet John Donne preached, "This only is charity, to do all, all that we can." Because we have not understood the necessity of living with thankful and generous hearts, we are less than whole people, unfulfilled in our spiritual yearning and disquieted within despite our general prosperity and affluence. The outward acts of generous giving and service are the key to inner peace and the meaning of life. This is stewardship of life, and, as we shall see, it is living in imitation of Christ as scripture enjoins us.

PERSONAL RELIGION

Religion, as I discussed in chapter 1, is what grasps and holds us, what directs the patterns of our living. It is the altar to which we bow down, however it may be defined. For some, it may be the dominating and painful addiction to alcohol or gambling which monopolizes and controls their days and nights. It may be an all-consuming hobby or artistic preoccupation which governs their every waking moment. "I live for golf or fishing," says one. Another exclaims, "My whole life revolves around my painting." The life of the saint, in contrast, is wholly occupied by the pursuit of the will of God. The predominant enterprise of many Americans and First World societies of this century, as we have seen, is the religion of materialism: the relentless quest for goods, property and possessions. As at no other time and like no other country in history, America has excelled in the quest, becoming a society of superabundance, ever acquiring and receiving, ever defending and retaining, often at the expense of others. In the midst of poverty next door and abroad, and by any measure, standard or statistic, American Christians are people of wealth and property. This is the focal point of our need for a religious conversion to a life of stewardship.

Whatever in life you give your heart to, that is the location of your treasure. It follows, then, that where your heart and your treasures lie, there is your god and that which you worship. In a materialistic and acquisitive culture such as ours, our hearts lie in the material gain and possessions we pursue. Men and women are valued and ranked according to their wealth and ability to amass fortunes. They are admired and achieve stature through possessions, as evidenced by the June 1987 report by CBS that twenty-four of the one hundred members of the U.S. Senate are now millionaires or mega-millionaires. The number of American millionaires is no longer newsworthy, since there are so many. Instead, in a recent story Associated Press business writer Rich Gladstone wrote about the fifty-six American billionaires, one of whom, with a net worth of $8.5 billion, is worth more than the gross national product of many Third World countries.

In working with congregations for over a decade, I have asked worshipers or group participants to raise their hands if they considered themselves to be living at or near the poverty level by American standards. I have yet to see the first hand lift or even jerk in hesitation. To be sure, small numbers of the poor are members of our congregations, and it is our responsibility to care for them and alleviate their condition. Some may say, "Well, you're looking at the wrong congregations or denominations," and admittedly this is addressed to mainline American churches. Generally speaking, however, members of the mainline Protestant denominations are people of means, especially when measured against any world standard of material attainment. Goods and property have come with great profusion to them and to others of the First World; our cups have overflowed, we have worked hard at it with a religious intensity. For these gifts not to be curses in disguise, we must learn to become generous stewards in the face of our common humanity with all people of our planet.

It is instructive to note that the New Testament does not categorically condemn wealth and prosperity. While to Jesus the relationship between people and possessions was one of the great priorities of the gospel, and although he frequently warned of the perils of prosperity's corrupting and mesmerizing powers, he did not indict wealth as evil, nor did he exalt poverty as virtuous. If the rich man in the parable who ignored the beggar Lazarus had responded to the need at his gate, the story may have had a more positive outcome; it would not be impossible for a man of wealth to enter the kingdom, just difficult, as difficult as a camel passing through a needle's eye (Mark 10:25). The Rich Fool (Luke 12:16–21) was foolish and lacked spiritual health because he could not let go and release his vast stores for the good of many. But he was not consigned to hell for his avarice and greed. Clearly, evil is not necessarily found in the acquisition of possessions and wealth; but it *is always* present in the greedy and unstewarded use of those gifts.

If the pursuit of material gain is not inherently evil, it is nonetheless true that the heart and its treasure must become vulnerable and open to the invasion of God the Giver and God's purpose for life. They cannot remain private and secret, exempt from or deaf to the call of stewardship. The whole person, including heart and treasure, is invited to participate in a life of contribution and giving, after the model of the triune God, who is revealed in every action and human understanding as Eternal Giver. This is the God who is known as the Creator Giver of Life, the Son who is given and who gives in total abandonment of self, and the Spirit who is revealed through the bestowal of gifts. Human creatures, in echo of our God-likeness, have integrity and meaning only to the extent that we become caretakers and stewards of the abundant and varied gifts we have freely received. Only then does the ethic of stewardship become operative and life-giving to the prosperous. We can have no spiritual depth or religious focus without sharing and being generous with gifts.

There are many things required of a life well lived and blessed materially. Surely one of them is to live with a thankful and generous heart. From persons who have little or nothing of the gifts of creation and life, generosity is less expected—although even then it is often found. Mark 12:41–44, frequently and mistakenly used as a defense for sparse giving to the church, is about Jesus who one day was watching at the temple treasure as the rich were bringing their gifts. A poor woman contributed two copper coins. Jesus commended her in the presence of the disciples because she gave everything she possessed, while the rich, who actually gave more, contributed less in proportion to their abundance. It is important to note that she is exalted and remembered not because she gave only two coins but because she gave everything she had. A similar example of total giving is told by Mother Teresa:

> On my first trip along the streets of Calcutta after leaving the Sisters of Loreta, a priest came up to me. He asked me to give a contribution to a collection for the Catholic press. I had left with five rupees, and I had given four of them to the poor. I hesitated, then gave the priest the one that remained. That afternoon the same priest came to see me and brought an envelope. He told me that a man had given him the envelope because he had heard about my projects and wanted to help me. There were fifty rupees in the envelope. I had the feeling, at that moment, that God had begun to bless the work and would never abandon me.[1]

The poor and those of meager estate can also give and be afforded the dignity of participation in redemptive causes. Often through the investment of our generous gift, however small, unexpected blessings are discovered.

A side effect of our affluence and abundance of gifts is the problem of holding and keeping them without stress and worry. That we face this difficulty is, in itself, a failure of stewardship. The magnitude of our prosperity can be understood by becoming familiar with new professional areas—financial planning consultants, wealth management services and comprehensive investment strategists in great numbers. The multiplication and management of wealth without worry or anxiety is a major American enterprise. The United States is the only country where financial and business matters are reported hourly as *news* by radio and television. An American who would be serious enough to ask, What can I possibly contribute to the world's well being while I live? should hear the clear answer: Out of the great and varied treasure with which you have been blessed, you can share liberally of yourself with an open and generous heart.

At a recent conference of churches held on the campus of a wealthy university, we delegates learned that there would be a "sacrificial lunch" one day, in response to the needs of world hunger. The sacrificial meal consisted of whole grain breads, varieties of cheese, a rich soup chock full of meat and vegetables, milk, coffee and sparkling cold water. We wondered where the sacrifice was in a meal that would have been a feast for anyone in the Third World. In America today the misconception leading to this meal is understandable. The conference of mainline churches was comprised of people who are comfortable and materially blessed, meeting on the campus of a university whose students learn more about acquisition than about sacrifice. By their norms the meal was, indeed, sacrificial. Such is America's difficulty in stewarding its vast and plenteous gifts.

Students today learn nothing about stewardship or generous giving. It is not part of the curriculum or the vocabulary, even, for the most part, in Christian seminaries. Although stewardship is a buzz word in business and politics, the average student is totally unfamiliar with it. Over the past twenty years the University of California and the American Council on Education have been tracking attitudes of college students. Overwhelmingly the goal of students today is wealth, not enlightenment. The study showed that in 1967 more than 80 percent of students said that their top priority was to "develop a meaningful philosophy of life." In 1987, 75 percent said their main goal was to "be well-off financially"—probably by age thirty-five. Colleges recognize that their appeal to students today lies in the "trade school" that heads them toward economic prosperity rather than in the liberal arts forum, which is the marketplace of ideas. From childhood we have learned to save (the child savings account and the piggy bank) and to spend, but rarely have we been taught to give. If a well-turned student of the late-twentieth century has not been taught the principle of stewardship and giving with a thankful heart his or her education has been flawed.

Sharing of wealth is the American Christian's assignment to the world of our time. Certainly, the church's call is to be servant of others, bearing the gifts of life. Were we one day to become stripped of wealth and impoverished, then the call to a faithful response could be in an area other than the relationship to goods and money. In our time, the Christians of poorer nations are often called as stewards of courage in the midst of economic injustice or to nonviolent resistance in the presence of racism and oppression. But so long as our present condition of superabundance continues, the proper stewarding of material gifts on behalf of all humankind is our call.

Religion prevails most strongly when we allow it to touch those things we most cherish, most treasure and hold closest to the heart. Whatever our priorities are, our investments and commitments of all kinds—emotional, intellectual, artistic, material—it is here that religion must apply if the spirit is to pervade and give life. What are the consuming efforts, passions, directions of one's life? If religious orientation does not impinge upon these areas, the religion is marginal and with perfunctory meaning.

This is why any serious religious quest is so difficult. Our deepest self yearns for spiritual meaning, but we check and suppress the hunger, protecting and keeping inviolate the places of our treasure. Then stewardship calls us to open our hearts, to expose our gifts and treasures, our strongholds and stores of bounty. Stewardship has a stake in everything that we value, that in proportion to its abundance it may be offered up as a sacred gift in thanksgiving and gratitude to the Source. Jesus claims us not in the peripheral and superficial areas of our life but at the very center where our treasures and prizes are to be found. As we respond freely and generously, yielding our strengths, the life of the spirit begins to open to us.

The invitation to the steward is simply to be faithful to the likeness of God in which we have been created (Gen. 1:26). In our imitation of the divine, we are called (1) to act as God has acted for us in creation; (2) to give and yield ourselves for others as Christ gave and yielded himself, and (3) to bear and steward gifts as the Spirit has gifted us. This invitation is underscored for us in 1 John 4:19: "We love, because he first loved us." As God has acted toward us, so we act toward God and the world. "Beloved, if God so loved us, we also ought to love one another" (1 John 4:11). In reflecting the likeness of God within us, the writer persuades us, "By this we may be sure that we are in him: he who says he abides in him ought to walk in the same way in which he walked" (1 John 2:5b–6). And, in 1 John 3:16–18, the writer most compellingly urges the gifted steward,

> By this we know love, that he laid down his life for us; and we ought to lay down our lives for the brethren. But, if anyone has the world's goods and sees his brother in need, yet closes

his heart against him, how does God's love abide in him? Little
children, let us not love in word and speech, but in deed and
in truth.

When in the presence of prayer, your own or someone
else's, freely spoken or read, note how often the words
"give," "gifts" and "thanks" or their derivatives occur. They
are more frequently heard than any other verb or noun
when discussing God's gracious action and our generous
response.

We are most faithful to our God-likeness when we endlessly bestow our generous gifts of grace, good will and
goods upon the world's need. To briefly describe the steward's vocation, we look to Paul's letter to the Philippians:
"Have this mind among yourselves, which you have in
Christ Jesus" (2:5). Although formed in the likeness of
God, do not pretend to be God, but begin the practice of
dispossession, taking the vocation of a steward, the proper
stance of the human being (Phil. 2:6–7; paraphrase).

Is the practice of stewardship essential to understanding
and living the Christian faith today? Is it the key to new
relevancy for mainline American churches and others?
Theodore Hesburgh retired in 1987 after a long and dis-
tinguished tenure as president of the University of Notre
Dame. Probably the most renowned living symbol of
scholarship and community-mindedness, he has received
112 honorary degrees from colleges and universities and
countless awards for excellence and public service. Father
Hesburgh has named two tasks to which he will give his
life in postretirement. They are the abolition of nuclear
weapons and the elimination of world poverty. Both are
redemptive tasks for the Christian American; each hinges
on the stewardship of resources, the use rather than misuse of gifts and the caretaking of our abundance.

3.

GOD
THE ENDLESS GIVER

The Lord's goodness surrounds us at every moment.
I walk through it almost with difficulty,
as through thick grass and flowers.[1]
—R. W. Barbour

To understand self and community from the perspective of stewardship, we must recognize that the God of our biblical understanding is primarily known to us as Eternal Giver. We live toward God and creation as the recipients of gifts at every turn, gifts that are uninvited, unexpected and undeserved. The way in which we consciously live in awareness of and response to these unmerited gifts is the record of our stewardship.

DIVINE GIFTS AND RECEPTION

From a biblical standpoint, we first become aware of God as the Giver of creation, the Giver of life who "calls the worlds into being." Ours is not the god who is known through collections of wise sayings or the denial of life, as in some Eastern religions. Nor is our God understood primarily by a set of divine attributes—omnipotence, omnipresence or omniscience, for example—although God may, indeed, incorporate these qualities. Rather, God is revealed to those in the Judeo-Christian tradition through the way in which God deals with God's people. The record of these dealings and this relationship is our biblical story.

When there was only darkness and the earth was without form, God gave creation and bestowed its care and management, as a gift, on humans whom God formed in God's own likeness. In that we have been created in God's likeness, we are called as co-creators and caretakers to be stewards of God's endless gifts. The gifts are not given once and for all; instead, from the Source there is a continuous and eternal outpouring of old and new gifts, which ever enrich and extend the creation process.

In receipt of God's manifold gifts, we must be ever mindful of the relationship between the Creator Giver and the creature caretaker. Misunderstanding our call to stewardship, we often assume the status of creator and sovereign and believe that our own hands and efforts are responsible for the gifts of life. But those who regard themselves as *self-made* suffer from mistaken identity. James 1:16–18 addresses this presumption of the steward to become the Sovereign:

> Make no mistake, my friends. All good giving, every perfect gift, comes from above, from the Father of the lights of heaven. With him there is no variation, no play of passing shadows. Of his set purpose, by declaring the truth, he gave us birth to be a kind of first fruits of his creatures. (NEB)

Humans are of the highest order of God's gifts, but the roles of Creator Giver and creature caretaker are never to be confused. Making that arrogant presumption would be a clear rejection of our call to stewardship.

In Paul Tillich's masterful collection of sermons, *The Eter-*

nal Now, there is a meaningful prayer. The opening lines of the prayer are a call to remembrance of the relationship between the Giver and caretaker.

> Almighty God! We raise our hearts to Thee in praise and thanks. For we are not by ourselves and nothing is ours except what Thou hast given us. We are finite; we do not bring anything into our world; we shall not take anything out of our world. Thou has given us the life which is ours, so long as it is Thy Will. We thank Thee that we have being, that we share in the inexhaustible riches of life, in the smallest and in the largest part of it. We give thanks to Thee when joy fills our hearts.[2]

God the endless Giver; humans the stewarding receivers. Ever distinct. Tillich's prayer bears witness to this relationship and to the purpose of life, filled as it is with the words *gifts* from God, and *thanks* from humans.

We have an insatiable appetite for God's gifts of creation; we collect and accumulate often to the point of greed and avarice. Addressing and countering this human tendency toward acquisition and power are the biblical accounts of the Tower of Babel in Genesis 11 and, interestingly, the Ten Commandments given to Moses and Israel. When viewed from the standpoint of stewardship, at least eight of the Decalogue have strong implications for that subject. Excluding the third commandment, which forbids taking God's name in vain, and the fifth, which commands the honoring of parents, the commandments contain strong elements of stewardship. The first forbids the worship of other gods including the god of mammon; the second speaks against graven images or molten idols of the substance of creation. The fourth commandment, about remembering and honoring the sabbath, commends the stewardship of days and time. The sixth, in behalf of the stewardship of all life, forbids killing. The seventh commandment, which speaks against adultery, calls us to be stewards of our love commitments, and the eighth condemns stealing in the interest of the stewardship of goods and property. The ninth prohibits false witness in our duty to be stewards of truth. Clearly an issue of stewardship, the tenth commandment enjoins us not to covet, desire or lust after that which is our neighbor's. The Creator gives life and its gifts but also orders its stewardship according to God's intention and plan for creation.

Clearly, God is not an abstraction or a static power in isolated heavenly splendor; God is dynamic and actively present and is made known to us primarily as the Giver of creation and life. Joseph Sittler suggests that Christian ethics and morality grow "out of the fact and the content of the endlessly giving God." He writes, "The Christian is to accept what God gives as Creator: the world with its needs, problems and possibilities; the revelation of this world as the creature of its faithful Creator with its given orders—family, community, state, economy. Each of these is invested with the promise and potency of grace, and each of these is malleable to the perverse purposes of evil."[3] The person of faith thankfully receives the gifts of grace, to use or misuse as he or she is wont to do, but always under the calling to be the responsible steward of God's abundant, unceasing gifts.

JESUS AS GIFT

God's self-disclosure unfolds in the new covenant through the coming of Jesus Christ, where Giver Creator meets creature caretaker in the human's own form. As the gospel story develops, the most striking characteristic is that the pattern of revelation is unchanged: God, in Christ, continues to be known primarily as Giver, having given the Son to the world (John 3:16) in a supreme gift of total grace.

How can we capture the spirit of the life and ministry of Jesus, in whom God meets us in a dynamic human presence? One way is to enter the mind of Christ Jesus, as Paul invites us in his letter to the Philippians (Phil. 2:5-9), the great passage of God's own stewarding of divine power through the gift of Christ. Ponder the passage again in the Phillips translation and hear what it says about stewardship:

> For he, who had always been God by nature, did not cling to his privileges as God's equal, but stripped himself of every advantage by consenting to be a slave by nature and being born a man. And, plainly seen as a human being, he humbled himself by living a life of utter obedience to the point of death. (Phil. 2:5-9)

The story of Jesus can be faithfully told in terms not only of God's supreme gift but of Christ the ultimate giver. In him is the fullest possible example of the meaning and invitation to stewardship.

> Do you remember the generosity of Jesus Christ, the Lord of us all? He was rich, yet he became poor for your sakes so that his poverty might make you rich. (2 Cor. 8:9 Phillips)

At the core of the Christian faith is the matter of coming to terms with gifts, giving and generosity. It is there in the very life, passion and death of Jesus Christ.

In his excellent volume, *The Meaning of Gifts*, the Swiss psychotherapist Paul Tournier writes about life's supreme gift.

> The great gift, the unique and living one, is not a thing but a person. It is Jesus Christ himself. In him God has given himself, no longer just things which he creates or has created, but his own person, his own suffering, and his own solitude, given unto death itself. He declared it himself, just before turning to face his cross, "Greater love has no man than this, that a man lay down his life for his friend" (John 15:13 RSV). This gift of all gifts is the self-commitment of God himself, who

31

> carried it through to the bitter end so that we may entrust ourselves to it. The almost unbelievable news of the revelation is that it really is a gift. It is free, without reservation and without recall.[4]

Psychologically this is what the meaning of gifts among humankind reveals to us, he insists. "Persons need to give because they need to give themselves, and all their gifts are signs of that deep-seated and universal desire to give oneself. To live is to commit oneself."[5]

As Jesus stripped and emptied himself in total dispossession, the picture of God the Endless Giver is drawn into sharp focus. We, as late-twentieth-century Christians, can only echo Paul's responsive exclamation in 2 Cor. 9:15 as it is variously translated: "Thanks be to God for his inexpressible gift!" (RSV); "Thank God, then, for his indescribable generosity to you!" (Phillips); "Thanks be to God for his gift beyond words" (NEB). The Christian should live in a state of constant joy and thanksgiving, which adversity cannot destroy, and respond with grateful and generous heart and hands to life and its servant needs.

THE HOLY SPIRIT: GIFT AND GIVER

This picture is further reinforced as we see God dealing with people through the third person of revelation, the Holy Spirit. The festival of Pentecost might well be described as the first day of new gifts from God. It is a new manifestation of the active, present God. What form shall this manifestation take? How shall we recognize this presence? It is seen in gifts of every kind and for every use as they are bestowed upon the creature-caretaker.

The Spirit came as "the rush of a mighty wind" (Acts 2:2), and the first gift of the Spirit was to give the faithful disciples the ability to communicate the Good News in the various languages of the throngs in Jerusalem. The prophecy of Joel 2:28–29 was being fulfilled in their midst as the Holy Spirit was poured out upon all, young and old, women and men, and as Peter directed the faithful to "repent and be baptized in the name of Jesus Christ for the forgiveness of your sins; and you shall receive the gift of the Holy Spirit" (Acts 2:38). Two key words, "forgive" and "gift," describe the acts of granting forgiveness and gifting humans with the Spirit by an endlessly giving and all-generous God.

The epistles speak clearly and frequently about the presence of the Holy Spirit in terms of giving and gifts. Paul wrote to the Corinthians,

> Now concerning spiritual gifts, brethren, I do not want you to be uninformed. . . . Now there are varieties of gifts, but the same Spirit; and there are varieties of service, but the same Lord; and there are varieties of working, but it is the same God who inspires them all in everyone. To each is given the manifestation of the Spirit for the common good. (1 Cor. 12:1, 4–7)

When one thinks about the biblical presence of the Spirit of God, it is in the sense of the Spirit endowing humans with gifts of many forms and rich variety.

GIVER CREATOR AND CREATURE CARETAKER

Just as God in every manifestation is characterized as the divine Giver of gifts, so the creature of God's own likeness is called to respond in kind—"for the common good." Gifts are not given so much for our pleasure, personal consumption or accumulation as they are intended to be generously used in the furthering purpose of creation. In Romans 12 (Phillips), Paul underscores this point. The great chapter is a handbook for the steward, the creature caretaker, on how to respond to and manage gifts. Paul exhorts,

> With eyes wide open to the mercies of God, I beg you my brothers [sisters], as an act of intelligent worship, to give him

33

your bodies, as a living sacrifice, consecrated to him and acceptable by him. Don't let the world around you squeeze you into its own mold, but let God remake you so that your whole attitude of mind is changed. Through the grace of God, we have different gifts.

"Let us use them," we are told. The gifts described, the extent defined, "freely" with "liberality," "give all, without limit." The task of the steward and the wide bounds of stewardship are fleshed out.

Speaking of gifts and the response to them, Joseph Sittler writes,

> The Christian is to accept what God gives as Holy Spirit, the Sanctifier. This acceptance includes the gifts that God gives from above, and the tasks which God gives in the world around. These gifts and these tasks belong together. The gift is celebrated in the doing of the task; the task is undertaken in faith as witness to the gift.[6]

God is not only the Giver; from out of the gifts God calls those in God's *likeness* to be stewards of other boundless gifts, to respond generously to tasks of creation and redemption.

4.

GENEROUS HEARTS AND PERSONAL POSSESSIONS

Not even You,
with your irresistible look
of infinite goodness,
succeeded in moving
the heart
of the rich young man.
And yet he, from his childhood,
had kept
all the commandments.
Lord, my Lord, may we never,
out of mistaken charity,
water down
the terrible truths
You have spoken to the rich.[1]
—Dom Helder Camara

The late Episcopal bishop James A. Pike urged churches and people toward a faith that held "fewer beliefs, more belief."[2] After many years in Christian ministry, I have reformed and redefined my own convictions, so that I carry much less religious baggage than I once did. My own statement of faith is now more lean and spare and holds fewer certainties.

H. L. Mencken, the great writer and newspaperman, who was known for his atheism and his frequent taunts against organized religion, was asked in an interview toward the end of his life, "If, after you die, you find yourself before the judgment seat and the twelve apostles, what will you do?" A thoughtful Mencken replied, "I would say, 'Gentlemen, I apologize. I was wrong.'" A vital sense of stewardship is so important to the faith and life that if, when we die, we find ourselves before the twelve apostles, their first question to us will probably have nothing to do with our church relationship, how often we prayed, or whether we obeyed the Ten Commandments or believed in the Apostles' Creed. Their first question will probably be, What did you contribute to life and to humankind?

Among my lean catalog of beliefs is one I hold with more certainty as time passes but which is not spoken of or written about very much, and is, in fact, quite unpopular. Preachers don't like to speak about it very much, nor do people wish to hear about it. The conviction is that at the very heart of the Christian faith is the matter of stewardship, which so dominates the two great testaments of our Scripture. What do I do with the gifts that I have received in life? How do I respond to and come to terms with my various gifts, including the gift of life, and the communal gifts of nature—earth, water, air, natural resources? How do I steward my relationship with other beings, human and earthly creatures? The answer is as all-inclusive and sweeping as Albert Schweitzer's own stewardship response, one of the greatest holistic stewardship concepts of all time: "reverence for life."

HOLISTIC STEWARDSHIP

In the summarizing passage of the three Synoptic Gospels (Mark 12:28–34, Matt. 22:34–40, Luke 10:25–28), Jesus gives the commandment that is the basis of all of the law and the prophets:

> You shall love the Lord your God with all your heart, with all your soul, with all your mind and with all your strength; and you shall love your neighbor as yourself.

This is a stewardship passage! Love is a verb; it is something you do! It is *active love* or *charity* (Latin *caritas*); simply, love applied. It is love as managed, employed and used for God and all creation. Human beings have a limitless capacity for giving and receiving love, but we do so hide and hoard it! Jesus commands that we love with the totality of the self in heart, soul, mind and strength—or in our giving, our doing and our being. The response of the creature caretaker is clearly to be a faithful steward of active love toward God and neighbor.

The steward is one who, within his or her own human limitations, seeks to imitate the fullness of God as Creator, Redeemer, Sustainer, by responding to the command to love totally with an open and generous heart. The faithful steward follows the lead of the Creator-Redeemer-Sustainer, all names synonymous with *givers of gifts*. So we are directed primarily in the epistles to follow by imitation.

> Therefore be imitators of God, as beloved children. And walk in love, as Christ loved us and gave himself up for us, a fragrant offering and sacrifice to God. (Eph. 5:1–2)
>
> Be imitators of me, as I am of Christ. (1 Cor. 11:1)
>
> Beloved, if God so loved us, we also ought to love one another. (1 John 4:11)
>
> We love, because He first loved us. (1 John 4:19)

As the Eternal One was, is, and will be, so are we the stewards in the time of our life.

Stewardship, then, is an activity and concept of vast implications that affects every area of life. The steward is a manager, a caretaker, a tender who imitates and acts in behalf of the God of life. In my argument, I will consider not always the whole of stewardship, but more often some of its parts. Everything relating to goods and possessions is a matter of stewardship. However, stewardship entails far more than the issue of possessions and money. Stewardship extends to all creation. Wherever faithful stewardship fails, all of creation suffers. Stewardship is about global resources: environment, ecology, economy, energy. It is about hunger, poverty, wealth, overabundance and the accompanying justice issues: world population, the farm crisis in America and the food chain, for example. And, of course, our stewardship of creation for the love of God and neighbor, as tenders of earth and space, we must deal with the issues of war, nuclear or conventional, and peace.

STEWARDSHIP: GENEROUS HEARTS

At the risk of too strictly limiting the concept of stewardship, I want to say that stewardship means living with a grateful and generous heart. The end, the goal of all Christian teaching, all prayer, all study of Scripture, all theologizing is to live with open, grateful and generous hearts. This message is at the apex of the gospel message. Even the fundamentalist's proof text says it for God's ultimate response to creation: "God so loved the world that he gave . . ." (John 3:16). It is important to note that it is not out of abundance that God gave, there being only one self to give, but God gave God's *only* Son. Giving with a generous heart is the kernel of wheat separated from the chaff.

Surely, we need the chaff to have the kernel, but the kernel is the essence. It is the pearl of great price, the one thing needed to live toward all of life, toward God and toward our neighbor, with a grateful and generous heart.

I am convinced that this is the only theme to preach from our pulpits today. Everywhere I look, at the texts and the lectionary, I see stewardship implications and occasions to proclaim living with grateful and generous hearts. So whether the season be Advent, Christmas, Lent, Easter, Pentecost, or Trinity, the sermon can contain the message of living with grateful and generous hearts. The sacraments, marriage, a funeral, Thanksgiving, a church anniversary require the same message: living with thankful hearts and generosity.

In our journey of life, our quest for meaning and purpose in our spiritual pilgrimage, the test is in how we relate to our gifts, our possessions, how we spend our life, how we invest it. Remember the wealthy young man who came to Jesus and asked, "What must I do to win eternal life?" Together they reviewed his religious experience, and he was found to be a solid young man of faith. But Jesus scrutinized him further and found one vital thing lacking. He told the young man, "Sell all of your possessions and distribute the money to the poor, and come and follow me." The young man lacked one thing—a grateful and generous heart! His spirit sank and he turned away in great distress because he had many possessions (Luke 18:18–27). Jesus had more to say in the gospels concerning wealth and possessions than about any other single subject. It is at the core of the Christian's faith response.

GENEROSITY: MISUNDERSTOOD AND MISPLACED

Looking at one's faith stance from this perspective and considering the relative affluence of Americans, we can recognize that the members of our churches are not generous. In 1986 the members of twenty-nine American denominations gave less than $280 per capita, including $66 for benevolences (mission beyond the local church) for the year.[3] If we were to stand before Jesus and report our faith response relative to our possessions, most of us would be embarrassed by our lack of generosity.

Financial statistics of per member contributions in American churches are, however, but an example, as revealing as they may be. The point is church membership, attendance at worship, Bible study, prayer and organizational activity mean nothing in our spiritual development until our possessions are touched and we attain generosity. Put bluntly, if you want to conduct a personal spiritual checkup, don't just count the Sundays you are in church or the church work that you do. Rather, examine your checkbook register and see where your priorities lie. Generosity need not be practiced only toward the church; it must move beyond the self and toward others. Perhaps the quest for meaning in life begins not with spiritual depth but with generosity.

Theologians Phillip and Phoebe Anderson once observed, "It may be easier to act yourself into a new way of thinking than to think yourself into a new way of acting. Our children may well learn what Christians *do* before they learn what the Christians *think*." It could be that *generosity done* precedes depth of *spirituality discovered*. Usually, we reverse the order, saying, "When I become more of a true believer, then I will become more generous in my faith response." If the young man in Luke 18 had begun by allowing his wealth to be vulnerable, he may have found the answer to his question about gaining eternal life.

Am I suggesting that it is possible to buy one's way to eternal life? No. However, we will never discover what eternal life is without a grateful and generous heart. A leader of a local church recently came to speak with me after a stewardship workshop. "This is interesting," he said, "but you know, I once was a member of another church and all they talked about was money. So we changed and came over to St. Luke's." Obviously, at St. Luke's a person could become a member, rise to the highest leadership position, and never have his faith response reach into his *sanctum sanctorum*—the sacred place of personal possessions.

It is not possible to reach any degree of spiritual maturity without a thankful and generous heart. Surely this is true for the vast majority of North Americans. The clue is in the word of Jesus in the Sermon on the Mount.

> Do not lay up for yourselves treasures on earth, where moth and rust consume and where thieves break in and steal but lay up for yourselves treasures in heaven for where your treasure is, there will your heart be also. (Matt. 6:19–21)

Wherever we decide to invest our treasures of whatever sort—our gifts, talents, time, energy, interest, love, wealth and possessions—that is the place where our heart will be found. And for most of us, our treasure is in the wealth that we have acquired or that we desire.

If wealth and possessions become our passion and we invest in ourselves and the things money can buy for us, we can be sure they will capture our heart and bind it in an inextricable web. John Wesley said: "When I have any money, I get rid of it as quickly as possible, lest it find a way into my heart." We can be a part of the church, but if our heart is not in it, it is probably because we have invested our treasure somewhere else.

MATURE GIVING

A most important task of the church is to lead persons who wish to follow the way of Jesus Christ to a state of thankful generosity. According to Hilbert J. Berger, the stewardship consultant, becoming Christian is a matter of growth, not unlike the human cycle from infancy to adult maturity. A young baby can readily clutch and grasp, at a mother's finger or a father's eyeglasses, but can not easily let go since the psychomotor skills have not developed to the point of allowing release. Little children are essentially on the receiving end of life. As Christians-to-be, we are all takers, keepers and holders. The words *me* and *mine* form a large part of our understanding. Berger suggests that a key mark of Christian maturity is becoming a giver. It is learning that release and generosity is the way to discover meaning and spiritual depth. In place of the clenched and clutching fist of the baby is the open and outstretched hand of the mature and generous giver who therein finds peace and meaning.

We must address the question Carl Sagan has raised: "Do you dare to believe that your personal significance in creation is in what you 'contribute' to meaning, to the hope of the future?" Our significance is not in how much we accumulate, not in getting to the top, not in the size of the estate we will leave, not in our name. Rather, we must ask, What did I contribute, here, in the time of my life? If we find ourselves before the twelve apostles, it may be the only question asked of us. Were we faithful in contribution, in the stewardship of our gifts?

5.

GENEROUS HEARTS AND PERSONAL RELATIONSHIPS

The path to the deepest self-discovery and the utmost release lies within the twofold experience of knowing oneself loved with infinite love, and of giving love in return "with all the heart, soul, mind and strength."

—Lewis Sherrill

Living with a generous heart must include not only generosity with money and possessions but with human relationships and personal well-being. Faithful stewards of the self, who have their own enlightened best interests at heart (that is, being a whole person), release their "self" to and for others, recognizing that one's self is best served by giving that self. A symptom of much psychological and physical illness is withdrawing from others, pulling back from interpersonal relations which require self-giving. When we withdraw from others, we are less than whole persons because we are interdependent and intended for social intercourse. A symptom of illness, physical or mental, is withdrawal and loss of the capacity to give. Sin could be defined as the unwillingness or inability to give of the self and the self's possessions. Søren Kierkegaard called sin "shut-upness" in oneself. We are healthiest, most whole and practice stewardship when we give and release the self for others. The greatness of Jesus lies in his identification as "the man for others."

In *The World As I See It*, Albert Einstein made an important statement about the stewarding of self.

> From the point of view of daily life, without going deeper, we exist for our fellow men—in the first place for those on whose smiles and welfare all our happiness depends, and next for all those unknown to us personally with whose destinies we are bound up by the common tie of sympathy. A hundred times every day I remind myself that my inner and outer life depend on the labors of other persons, living and dead, and that I must exert myself in order to give in the same measure as I have received and am still receiving.[1]

Einstein looked deeply and perceptively into life and unlocked some of the universe's greatest secrets, yet he simply and profoundly saw that receiving gratefully from others prompts a corresponding generosity of self-giving.

Personal wholeness and well being can be measured to an extent by the ability to give oneself to others in significant and generous ways. When we can not, we become miserable and often need outside help. Much of counseling is about the stewardship of love and caring. An opening question a counselor may ask of one who is having difficulties in a relationship might be, What are your patterns of giving—of yourself, your gifts? This question is especially pertinent in regard to money and personal possessions. It has always been interesting to me that in personal or group counseling, people will talk about almost anything, openly and unashamedly. They will share intimacies about their sexual lives, personal problems and hangups, and private details about family situations. What they seldom do is share information about their personal wealth and their patterns of giving. Those are our most closely guarded secrets, and, because possessions and their pursuit so grip and entangle us, they are a source of psycho-spiritual dis-ease. Michel Quoist writes, "I am afraid of what I give. It hides what I withhold." Family wellness is often determined by how generous we are with our time and attention to our spouse and children. Because we are not naturally generous with affection, we need bumper stickers to ask us, Have you hugged your kids today? Your wife? Your cat? Stewardship is hugging and giving affection. If we invest the treasures of our selves in those to whom we are closely tied, there our heart will be also. Most of us are gifted with the capacity to give love and show care, but penurious about demonstrating it. We hoard it for many reasons and so, perhaps, it spoils and has a toxic effect on our own personality.

Misplaced generosity with treasure has serious results. A man was having great difficulty as the result of involvement in an extramarital relationship. A counselor finally led him to see that if he ceased investing his gifts of time, energy and interest in the other person, his heart would find release from the affair. Whatever we give ourselves to holds the attention of our hearts.

Beyond the question of to whom or to what we give our gifts and how generous we are, we must recognize that there are often things we hang on to that we need to give up or give away. There are grudges, resentments, bad will that we bottle up and hold onto until they fester in our hearts and make us ill. We say, I will never give in. I'll never forgive this or that person. This clutching and keeping of ill will is failed stewardship. Give it up!

In Matt. 18:21–22, the disciple Peter, believing himself open-hearted and forgiving, asked Jesus, "How often shall my brother sin against me and I forgive him? As many as seven times?" Jesus' reply advocated generosity in forgiveness: "I do not say to you seven times, but seventy times seven." He might also have said, "Freely you have received forgiveness, so freely give." In the stewardship of forgiveness, God's capacity for grace is greater than our capacity for sin. His well is deeper than our thirst. So, in our generous forgiveness, we become free of ill will and brokenness. Charlotte Armstrong gives us the insight in one of her novels: "To forgive is just to be healed of the hurt given. It is you who have to give up being hurt! Then, as you forgive, by the mercy of God you are healed. It is all tied together."

We can see how the concept and practice of giving are tied to psychological and spiritual health. This act of stewardship is almost always helpful and healthful: just complete the phrase as you wish, "I give my ———." I give my hand in friendship, or I give my love to you. Holding keys to full life are found in offering forgiveness, in giving away goods and possessions, in bestowing gifts. We are better and stronger when we give up fear, anger, grudges and resentments, and when we give out praise, offerings, bequests and honor. Personal and communal life thrive on self-giving and generous open heartedness.

Psychologically we are stronger and more in the condition of shalom when we can give generously even in small ways. Paul Tournier writes,

> Happy are those nations where the custom of gifts has remained a vital thing, unlike our lands [Western societies] which have been dried up by an industrial and bureaucratic civilization! This is what strikes us in the East and in Arab lands. When my son was in the hospital in Algiers, after an automobile accident, every one of the Algerians who came to see him brought him a gift. In Greece, we never went anywhere without being welcomed with a cup of Turkish coffee, a bitter orange, preserves, or some other treat. In Crete we visited strangers to us but to whom our Athenian friends had written of us. While in their home, I whispered to my wife,

"Look, what a beautiful cup!" Immediately the woman emptied it of the fruit that was in it, and handed it to us, "There! This is for you!" Yes, and she offered the fruit to us, too, as well as some other small gifts.[2]

And who was the greater beneficiary of joy and well being—the recipient or the giver?

Why is romantic love always so appealing in books, the movies or real life stories? Because there is so much giving and receiving involved. Even if for just a brief moment, what we observe and feel is beautiful and we yearn for it for ourselves or remember it. Romantic love at its best is many things and can be described in many ways, but it is primarily a matter of giving and receiving. Howard Thurman observed, "Love will make us give for someone what no power on earth could make us give or do if we did not love." I still return to one of my favorite touching examples of giving and receiving love from O. Henry's short story *The Gift of the Magi*. Two poor struggling young lovers want to gift each other at Christmas. He pawns his precious pocket watch in order to buy two jeweled combs for her long hair. She has her long hair cut and sold in order to purchase a beautiful watch chain for his gold watch, a tender and beautiful portrait of self-sacrifice for the object of one's love through the stewarding of each other's gifts.

I have observed many relationships over the years. Of particular meaning to me was the golden anniversary celebration of a remarkable survivalist couple who gathered with their large family and their friends. Dutch and Mary were a unique pair, with a splendid high-achieving family scattered around the states. Together, they were gracious and warmhearted, entertaining friends and serving church and community. But Dutch, a retired Santa Fe Railroad boss, could be cantankerous, explosive of temper and overbearing, often embarrassing others with his outbursts. The self-appointed, although diligent, steward of the large churchyard, he was feared by all the volunteers, who would want to be warned if Dutch was coming over that day. If you were on his wrong side or did not do it his way, there would be trouble. But Mary held him in her heart and gave herself, and it was beautiful to behold. She was gentle, yet strong; patient, but, after years as a teacher, not weakly submissive. At her death she was remembered not as a long-suffering wife but as one of those many saints who had put up with the likes of him all those years.

The secret of their tested relationship was that Mary gave her all to Dutch and their covenant. She did not seek to balance giving and receiving; she just gave and gave again. It is true that this kind of giving seems especially more the gift of women. But perhaps in and through that gift, we may become gifted ourselves in our ability to give more.

Some may argue that Mary's kind of giving was an undesirable, negative kind of giving on demand, almost a form of servitude and bondage—the kind of demeaning female obedience that was the norm when Dutch and Mary were young. But those people are wrong. I would answer their criticism by saying that when a voluntary, freely offered commitment was made by a spouse, mostly of former times, to give and to give again, it was usually the glue that held a relationship together for life. Giving does that.

How may we apply the lesson of Dutch and Mary—as dated and out-of-step as it seems with contemporary attitudes toward gender roles—to our lives? Today many marriages fail because neither partner is willing to give with the generosity that was once expected of at least one of the partners. True, it was usually the woman who did the giving—and that was unfair. But my point is that it was the *giving* that held the bond. Once women rightly became disinclined to do most of the giving, relationships began to fail with greater frequency.

As we strive for greater equality between the sexes, men must learn to give to the marriage relationship in ways with which they are not accustomed by cultural training or example, and women will need to give with similar generosity. For relationships to thrive, there must be a mutual outpouring of abundance in the stewardship of self-giving. Sometimes the world community, shaky as it is, survives on the giving of its saints, known and unknown, whose generosity of self redeems the avarice and greed of millions. This happens in large and small ways where great numbers are affected as well as where two or three are gathered in family.

And where is joy to be found in religious experience, that rare and elusive quality that is found in the promise of the gospel? Whatever else joy means, it is coupled closely with a grateful and a generous heart. Surely one of the reasons why Christmas is such a joyous season is because it is involved with gifts and giving. As we have received the gift of the Christ child, so we respond with generosity to one another in the season of open-hearted good will.

Rightly or wrongly, Christmas is the most widely observed and celebrated holiday of the year. We decry its commercialization, banality, tinsel and glitter, and the hype of Santa and Rudolph the Red-nosed Reindeer, but for many it is a time of generosity and gifts, of open-heartedness and joyous excitement. For both the wrong and right reasons, Christmas is about gifts and giving. People prepare gifts for loved ones and friends months in advance or at the last minute, but the meaning is caught up in the spirit of giving. The merchants rejoice, but so do churches because the best month of the year for benevolent giving is December. Every year, we read the same articles by psychologists and counselors who remind us that for many Christmas is the most depressing time of the year. Is this because giving is painful for many people, or because there is no one to give to or receive from? The depression may well be tied to a personal history related to past injuries or afflictions regarding either excessive or non-existent giving and receiving patterns. We would do well to ponder the significant meaning of gifts that is wrapped up in the meaning of Christmas. Why not share the Christmas spirit every day for the whole world?!

As the wise men quested and searched after the star, they found the great gift beneath it and "they rejoiced exceedingly with great joy" (Matt. 2:10–11). Note the emphasis—the magnitude of their joy over the gift of God. And what did they do in response to the gift? They rejoiced and fell to their knees paying the child homage. Then, they brought gifts. They opened their treasures and offered him gifts! Joy opens us to generosity, and we are most near to joy when we give.

God loves a cheerful giver because a giver is not cheerful until he or she is generous. Small gifts of any kind are begrudged, and there is no joy in them. The generous giver isn't cheerful with a kind of forced smile; the generous giver is cheerful because he or she can not contain the joy. It lights up the heart and the face. Did you ever give an extravagant gift to someone you cared about? You spent more than you should have, but you did it anyway. How did you feel when you gave that expensive, unexpected gift, and the recipient was unwrapping it? Well, that feeling continues to be one of the greatest experiences of life. The wonderful part is that the giver feels as much, perhaps more, joy than the receiver. The stewardship of giving gifts works that way.

In the story of Jesus and the woman of Bethany (Mark

14:3–9), we can wonder who experienced the greater sense of joy over an extravagant gift—Jesus, who received it, or the woman of Bethany, who gave it. When she broke open a flask of precious oil and poured it over Jesus in a beautiful and tender gesture of pre-anointing before death, some in the community were outraged at what they saw as waste. But Jesus praised her, rejoicing in the gift, and told them she would be remembered wherever the gospel was preached. Many times a thankful heart requires an extravagant, generous gift, given without regard to cost, as today the Missionaries of Charity of Calcutta say: "We receive everything free, we give everything free, purely for the love of God."[3]

The most marvelous commentary on the subject of giving is Charles Dickens' *A Christmas Carol,* the miracle story of a true conversion experience. Ebenezer Scrooge, the prosperous old skinflint, characterizes Christmas as a day that gives one an excuse to pick another's pocket, and he begrudges his bookkeeper, Bob Cratchitt, the day off from work. But in his Christmas sleep of apparitions, he acquires religion. Overwhelmed by joy, he is converted to generosity; and to the amazement and delight of everyone, his grateful heart is set free and his cup overflows. The new Scrooge is in a state of bliss, which is heaven, which is giving. The old man leaps about with the glee of a small boy, and when he discovers that it is yet Christmas Day, he eagerly opens the treasure of his heart, sharing his bounty with family and community. A new spirit of generosity and sharing has penetrated the very core of his being. The reader wants to dream on about the re-formation of Ebenezer Scrooge as the steward.

How do we respond in life to the people or occasions that we love? Whether it is a birthday, anniversary, holy day or holiday—always, it is with gifts. Celebrations bring joy and require gifts. Psalm 66:1–2 extols, "Make a joyful noise to God, all the earth; . . . *give* to him glorious praise."

A contemporary example of joy received through giving is seen in the Missionaries of Charity under Mother Teresa. The society affirms that, in order to know the poor, they must know what poverty is. The key to their communal life is their poverty, which is also their freedom, their strength and, profoundly, their joy. Mother Teresa says, in *My Life for the Poor,*

> The generous surrender of our young sisters and brothers is a most wonderful gift to God, to our society and the whole church. Many of our sisters come from well-to-do families. To see them just leave their life behind is something wonderful. What is very beautiful in the young people is their generosity. Very often we think that the young people are drawn to the *work,* but you would be surprised that they are drawn to the life of *poverty.* All our sisters are full of joy. They are the most striking example of living faith with joy.[4]

Many things may detract from joy in life, but selfishness and dysfunction in giving are obstacles to meaning. We simply are not designed that way. Our own best interests are served by self-giving in risky and generous ways. The expectant mother knows this in her heart. The woman in labor gives and risks the pain. But according to John 16:21, Jesus said, "When a woman is in travail, she has sorrow because her hour has come; but when she is delivered of the child, she no longer remembers the anguish for joy that a child is born into the world."

The gift of painful sacrifice intensifies the joy. We cannot be whole persons, nor can we fulfill God's intent for God's own partner, apart from living with a thankful and generous heart.

All good gifts around us come from You,
O, God.

GENEROUS HEARTS AND PERSONAL RELATIONSHIPS

You have given us life and new life in Christ.
As you have given us gifts,
so we offer our gifts
that we may be gifts to one another,
even as Jesus so taught and lived.
Amen.[5]

—Roger D. Knight

6.

THE SACREDNESS OF WORKS

The flowing out of God always demands a flowing back.
—Jan Van Ruysbroeck (1293–1381)

Cosmically and eternally, God generously gives every good and perfect gift, including the "only one of its kind" gift—God's Son. Jesus is who he is because he gave his life of abundance to emptiness and poverty and to death. And the Holy Spirit comes to us and dwells in us through rich varieties of gifts. Endless giving, in whatever manifestation, is God's clearest and most consistent act in the biblical story.

Again and again in the New Testament we, as faithful followers, are reminded of the strong identification between Christ's stewardship of life and our own. Jesus stripped himself of all gifts, chose to become poor and, finally, gave himself to suffering and death. We are invited, again as stewards of many gifts, to *Imitatio Christi*—the imitation of Christ, our proper stance before the Giver of Life. Not only does this serve the way of Christ in the world, but it is the means by which we attain unto wholeness and peace, as promised by the gospel. To the Ephesians it was written, "Therefore, be imitators of God, as beloved children. And walk in love, as Christ loved us and gave himself up for us, as a fragrant offering and sacrifice to God" (Eph. 5:1–2). Paul himself said to the Corinthians, "Be imitators of me, as I am of Christ" (1 Cor. 11:1). By imitation of Christ I do not mean to suggest "redoing" Christ; the work of salvation is done, as Christ died once and for all. Instead, alive on God's earth and with the model of Jesus before us, we are invited to participate in the process of creation and redemption, in the very Spirit and likeness of the all-giving God.

CALLED TO WORKS

Do not draw from this the idea that it is possible to earn grace and salvation and, through the exercise of faithful stewardship, merit God's gift of redemption. Scripture is clear: "For by grace you have been saved through faith; and this is not your own doing, it is the gift of God—not because of works, lest any [wo]man should boast" (Eph. 2:8, 9). We need yet another grace for salvation. It, too, is the gift of God and God alone. Nevertheless, in the very next verse the writer of Ephesians says in support of good works that we are "created in Christ Jesus for good works . . . that we should walk in them" (Eph. 2:10). Thus, while we are not saved by works, it is works to which we are called as stewards of gifts.

Defining how a Christian is to live and act in the modern world, Dietrich Bonhoeffer in *The Cost of Discipleship* speaks powerfully to the task:

> Those who follow Christ are destined to bear his image, and to be the brethren of the firstborn Son of God. Their goal is to become "as Christ". We become the sons of God, we stand side by side with Christ, our unseen Brother, bearing like him the image of God. A creature, and yet he is destined to be like his

Creator. Created man is destined to bear the image of uncreated God. His destiny is to bear this mystery in gratitude and obedience to his Maker.[1]

Bonhoeffer is quick to assert, though, that, "to be conformed to the image of Christ is not an ideal to be striven after."[2] Living in imitation of Christ is not a prize to be won, but a gift to be received. Because God the Giver gave us God-self in Christ, so we can give ourselves as Christ. God's gift enables the release of our gift. So, argues Bonhoeffer, "We cannot transform ourselves into his image; it is rather the form of Christ which seeks to be formed in us (Gal. 4:19), and to be manifested in us. Christ's work in us is not finished until he has perfected his own form in us. He has become like a man, so that men should be like him."[3]

Then, in an exalted passage, Bonhoeffer concludes,

> He is the only "pattern" we must follow. And because he really lives his life in us, we too can "walk even as he walked" (1 John 2:6), and "do as he has done" (John 13:15), "love as he loved" (Eph. 5:2/John 13:34; 15:12), "forgive as he forgave" (Col. 3:13), "have this mind which was also in Christ Jesus" (Phil. 2:5), and therefore we are able to follow the example he has left us (1 Peter 2:21), lay down our lives for the brethren as he did (1 John 3:16). It is only because he became like us that we can become like him. [4]

From our standpoint of abundance, if we know about the world's pain and brokenness, if we acknowledge it, but live in un-Christly ways, we cannot attain wholeness or find spiritual vitality. More than any other ethical response the only "pattern" we should follow is giving of self and wealth with a generous abandon.

The practice of stewarding gifts does not mean adhering to abstract and tidy propositions, nor affirming a catalogue of regulations and hardened duties. It is not having all the right answers in advance or saying the right things. Rather,

Christian stewardship is a dynamic action appeal to "put on Christ," to "be crucified with Christ," letting "his mind be in us" that we may freely and faithfully offer up ourselves as responsible stewards and servants of others in the give and take of life. Often our stewardship, conducted in imitation of Christ, will require hard decisions about issues such as peace and justice. It will involve working hard with all our resources deployed to build better relationships with others near and far. It will require the development of ways through our gifts, including moral persuasion, to feed the hungry, clothe the naked and house the unsheltered. It will mean acting and serving in the spirit of Christ with our time and energy in any area of life where we find his way to be unknown. Being blessed with gifts requires our generous offerings. Faithful stewardship of gifts is not for spectators of life or uninvolved bystanders; it is a generously active partnership between God the Giver and the creature caretaker, and it is the only way to spiritual renewal.

Catholic theologian Hans Kung in his study of the essence and form of the church, entitled *The Church*, examined the nature of ecclesiastical office as such, and after careful pursuit identified *diakonia*, or "service as the imitation of Christ" in behalf of humankind, as the essential element of ministry. He concluded,

> It is not law or power, knowledge or dignity, but "service" which is the basis of discipleship. The model for the disciples in their following of Christ is therefore not the secular ruler and not the learned scribe, nor even the priest who stands above his people; the only valid model is that of the person who serves at table: "But I am among you as one who serves" [at table] (Luke 22:27).[5]

We often pray, "Thy will be done on earth as it is in heaven." If God's will were to be done on earth, would we have heaven on earth? The idea of heaven on earth is elusive and difficult to conceptualize, but whether it is achievable or not, we must pursue the state wherein everyone is generous to others with a thankful heart and no one is in need. God the Giver looked at creation, including earth, and saw that it was good. Its intended goodness is worth every gift that we can steward to the attainment of that end.

Assisting persons first to admit, discover and claim their own gifts and then to release them with unleashed generosity is a clear task of the church. Our churches are filled with people who have gifts of many kinds, including spiritual gifts or charisma. If we believe in the gifts of the Spirit, then as churches we are charismatic communities, with a lower case "c." That ancient dynamic reality of the church, so rich in biblical grounding, must not be surrendered to the "pentecostals" and "charismatics." In the United Church of Christ's *Manual on Ministry* The Ordained Minister's Code states, "I will nurture and offer my gifts for ministry to the Church. I will seek to call forth and nurture the gifts of others in the Church and join their gifts with mine for the sake of the mission of Jesus Christ and the health of the church."[6] This commitment is what I write of here.

In reclaiming the gifts of the Spirit, our ministry is to *discover* gifts of which the holder may be unaware, *develop* gifts in their unrealized potential for service and *deploy* gifts where the need becomes clear. In imitation of God, each steward must be alert for the Spirit's gifts in self and others and, with thankful and generous hearts, must be ready to offer the gifts in mission and service to all of life after the model of the Giver. The call is clear: "Having gifts that differ according to the grace given to us, let us use them" (Rom. 12:6). Service to others is an aim of our stewardship. Again as Bonhoeffer wrote, "If we love, we can never observe the other person (or segment of society) with detachment, for he is always and at every moment a living claim to our love and service."

The offerings of faithful stewards are central to the idea of worship and the norm of the faith response in both the Old and New Testaments. Elaborate forms and manners of offering are described in exacting, often gory, detail in, for example, Exod. 29:38–46 and Numbers 28 and 29. The altar and its offerings became the meeting place between God the Giver and the creature caretaker,

> It shall be a continual burnt offering throughout your genera-
> tions at the door of the tent of meeting before the Lord, where
> I will meet with you, to speak there to you. There I will meet
> with the people of Israel, and it [the offering] shall be sancti-
> fied by my glory. (Exod. 29:42–43)

The psalms describe the righteous as those who are "generous and give" (Ps. 37:21b), and they continually speak of worship in terms of the bringing of gifts and offerings. "Ascribe to the Lord the glory due his name; bring an offering and come into his courts!" (Ps. 96:8). And, "With a free-will offering, I will sacrifice to thee; I will give thanks to thy name, O Lord, for it is good" (Ps. 54:6). And in the prophets, in what appears to be the rejection of substance offerings, Mic. 6:6–8 summarizes the manner of approaching the Lord in a total stewardship of self by doing justice and kindness and walking in humility with God. (I discuss Mic. 6:6–8 on pp. 109–10). None of these gifts or examples is compatible with withholding and keeping gain and possession for one's self.

When Jesus was born, the wise men, in the only re-
sponse they could give to the Child of God, fell down and worshiped him and, "opening their treasures, they offered him gifts . . ." (Matt. 2:11–12). Later, when Jesus cured a leper in one of the cities of Galilee, he told the man to go and make an offering for his cleansing (Luke 5:14). The

apostle Paul often wrote of offering as worship, "a sacrifice acceptable and pleasing to God" (Phil. 4:18), but nowhere more compellingly than in 2 Corinthians 9, which is devoted entirely to gifts and offerings. "You will be enriched in every way for great generosity, which through us will produce thanksgiving to God" (2 Cor. 9:11). Clearly, the only approach God's faithful stewards can take to God the Giver is prayer, humility and generous gifts.

A NEW SACRAMENT

The liturgical and actual symbol of giving in Christian worship is, of course, the offering, or the service of giving. Traditionally in worship, when Holy Communion is celebrated, the offering takes place just before the sacrament; and often the Communion elements are brought forward to the table or altar immediately before the Eucharistic celebration. In the offertory, the bread and the wine, along with the monetary gifts, are offered up to God for consecration in a most solemn manner. When Holy Communion is not celebrated, the monetary offering is presented in the same way, usually accompanied by a prayer of consecration or dedication. There is a profound interconnectedness between the sacrament of God's gift to us and the creature caretaker's worldly gift, here, financial gifts, humble and lowly, but given in behalf of all creation in the very likeness of God. The association between the eternal mysteries of God in the sacrament and the faithful stewarding of the material stuff of creation is made by Mother Teresa:

> In the Eucharist I see Christ in the appearance of bread. In the slums I see Christ in the distressing disguise of the poor. The Eucharist and the poor are but one love for me.[7]

A phrase from the Eucharistic prayer of the United Church of Christ's *Book of Worship* is most appropriate.

Offered prior to the distribution of the communion elements, the prayer gives thanks "for the beauty and bounty of the earth" and appeals "for the vision of the day when sharing by all will mean scarcity for none."[8] Then, in the midst of this plea for faithful stewardship, the sacrament is given and received for our nourishment.

In the mainline Protestant churches, one of the changes brought about by the sixteenth-century Reformation was the recognition of but two sacraments—baptism by water and Holy Communion. Not only were they both instituted by Jesus Christ himself, but they represent the beginning and the continuing of our life in the faith. (Roman Catholics, of course, have seven sacraments, the other five—confirmation, marriage, ordination, penance, and last rites—are regarded as rites of the church by most Protestants.)

I take this moment to dare to suggest that we regard the offering as a sacred obligation, a third sacrament—the sacrament of the Offering. Would we have the temerity (or the courage) to amend or alter our understanding of the sacraments, the most sacred ordinances of the church?

While I realize the almost certain impossibility of implementing my suggestion, perhaps by merely suggesting it I may encourage the reevaluation of the importance of the offering and its parallels with both baptism and Holy Communion. The sacraments have to do with tangible objects—water, bread, the fruit of the vine and, in this case, money! When properly used, each holds grace potential as sacred elements. While it is true that Christ instituted the two sacraments, he spent much of his ministry teaching about our relationship to money and possessions, which he, himself, gave up. Augustine and, later, the sixteenth-century reformers spoke of the sacraments as "a visible word," "a visible form of invisible grace" and "a visible sign of a sacred thing." Is there not a correlation between God the Giver of grace and the creature caretaker, a giver of gifts? Is not the offering a visible sign of a sacred thing, namely, the giving of gifts, the offering, the visible word of our faithful stewardship of gifts?

This came to me one day while I sorted the remnants and relics of a small disbanded congregation. The moment was sad, as I went through those once meaningful artifacts of the former church. There were flags and poles, a pulpit lamp, some linens. And then in a cardboard box I found the symbols of grace: the old, worn pulpit Bible, a brass table cross, the stained baptismal bowl and the communion ware—outward signs of Word and sacrament. Lastly, at the bottom of the box, lay a final piece, an offering plate. It was wooden, stained dark and bottomed by a shiny, well-worn circle of velvet. Over the years it had become nearly threadbare from receiving the gifts of the faithful. This worn offering plate touched me and has become a personal treasure which I sometimes carry as a symbol.

Why are the baptismal bowl and communion ware more cherished than the offering plate? The offering plate is the most feared and threatening symbol of the church. It is more feared than the cross, because the offering plate knocks at the door of the *sanctum sanctorum* in America, our heart of hearts, our most holy, guarded and secret place; it beckons to our treasure. In baptism and the Holy Communion, we receive the gifts of grace from God the Giver. In the offering we have the opportunity to respond and to exercise a measure of our stewardship. If our offering is a sacramental act, if it is serious and generous, then both receiving and giving will be exalted in the sacraments.

In the two traditional sacraments, God gives Godself to us. But every relationship requires give and take. The elements of the sacraments are for our consumption. We begin at baptism with a bowl of water and, if enough initial believers were present, we would empty all of the water in the bowl. At Holy Communion, we begin with a full chalice and plates heaped with bread or wafer; and, if enough are present, all is consumed. In the offering, we begin with an empty plate, and through our generous act, we should return it full in glad thanksgiving. Is not our stewardship act, through the offering, the symbolic response to God's grace and generosity? True worship is the alternating rhythm of consumption and contribution, receiving God's gifts of endless grace, giving generously of human gifts in like manner. It is coming to the font of blessing and to the bounteous table to accept God's benefits, and responding humbly, generously and with a thankful heart to the waiting plate. If we enter hungering and thirsting for righteousness, we are always filled; if we depart leaving a worthy gift of ourselves, we are satisfied and fulfilled. Here the full circle of receiving and giving, the cycle of creation, is practiced and celebrated. Our offering at worship represents what we think about God's gifts. As freely we have received, so freely let us give (Matt. 10:8).

The way in which we regard the offering in the liturgy of worship reflects our discomfort and unwillingness to deal openly and seriously with generous giving. We give less time and thought to planning and preparing for the offering than to any other part of the worship service. It has become a kind of dignified disguise for collecting money, usually preceded or followed by announcement time, the "lighter" time of worship, and filler music played to occupy the time the "collection" takes.

What we consistently bring as an offering is our most distinguishing mark as a Christian steward. That is why offering needs to be raised to the level of the sacramental, and thought of as a true act of worship, a costly response to God and to life. Unshackling people from penurious token-tipping and releasing them for joyous and generous contribution is a responsibility of American churches. Christianity is a burden as long as we are ungenerous, pinched and cramped in our giving. Our treasure must become vulnerable to release if religion is to become a joy. Generous givers rejoice in their faith because their hearts are part of their faith, following after their treasure. When true giving brings us to this level of spiritual development, offering becomes sacramental.

A test for measuring Christian maturity in faith is similar to the test that psychologist Abraham Maslow offered for mature adulthood: "When a person accepts a lifestyle that indicates they want to put more into life than they want to take out, they have reached adult maturity." Life is a matter of give and take, and the multigifted people of the First World have been on the lopsided *taking* end of life. But therein lies an amazing opportunity. By "putting on Christ" and modeling dispossession through faithful stewardship, the new day of "sharing by all, meaning scarcity for none" is before us. Giving and sharing by the wealthy of the world is the only path to spiritual discovery.

7.

THE AMERICAN CHURCH AND A MODEL COMMUNITY

> The World is too much with us; late and soon,
> Getting and spending, we lay waste our powers:
> Little we see in Nature that is ours.
> —William Wordsworth

While it is not intrinsically evil to seek and accumulate profit and possessions, I wonder whether the quest for wealth is compatible with the Christian faith. Can one be rich beyond basic comforts and needs and, at the same time, expect to know a life with spiritual meaning? Can we be whole persons in a climate of possessiveness in which we become consumed by material wants and pursuits? The charge has been made that people of the "mainline" Protestant churches, while trying to respond to an inner spiritual yearning, fail to discover its gift because they are overwhelmed by the weight of the religion of materialism and cannot hear the call to giving and generosity.

65

A CHURCH ADRIFT AND REFLECTING SOCIETY

It is one thing to recognize the absence of Christian stewardship in American society in general but quite another to remember the source of the idea of Christian stewardship and study its application by the mainline churches and their members. For the majority of American Protestants, the church and the practice of the faith are of marginal concern in the midst of the choices and demands set before them. For the average Christian, church is largely a matter of a Sunday morning experience and some other limited and sporadic commitments of time and personal involvement. The lack of financial support, an important measure of commitment, speaks for itself.

The *1988 Yearbook of American and Canadian Churches* reports that for the years 1986 and 1987 (various statistics are given for both years), forty-four American Protestant denominations and twenty-seven Canadian denominations gave an average per capita gift of $262.88, which includes $54.26 for benevolences. What does this say? The picture is dismal. There is no avoiding the fact that the church and religious faith expressions are not central in the life of the typical American Protestant. The faith and the church that represents it direct neither the patterns of our living and giving nor our personal stewardship. It is not that the church does not expect more from its members. Rather, the church does not even ask it, much less require it, because people simply do not respond. Indeed, they often become alienated and walk away. How people steward or fail to steward their lives and gifts is off-limits, private and inviolable. Our wealth and possessions are holding us captive, and, among other things, this is destroying the church.

I am not trying, here, to berate the church. It does seem to me, though, that the church is becoming a pathetic and impotent witness to the way of Jesus Christ. It is declining in membership and resources, and it does not have the means to carry out effectively its mission and message to the world. The church that I know is neither a significant spiritual presence nor an influence at home or abroad. And the often-sought solution—a different church or a new church—begs the issue. The issue is a renewed church. This matter of looking for a better church "out there somewhere" is absurd. No church has a corner on truth and practice, and many of them would serve anyone's needs well enough if taken seriously. A sixteenth-century reformer referred to his church as a mother who was a prostitute. But because she was his mother, he loved her nonetheless. We work in the midst of this tension between harlotry and faithfulness as the church comes to grips with its stewardship. A measure of God's gift of grace is God's tolerance of the church and its members in its present form and practice.

I believe the root of the problem in American mainline churches lies in our lifestyle—getting one's piece of the action, as much as one can, as fast as one can. Our approach too easily becomes "everyone for him- or herself," and no one for others. And increasingly since 1945, although the number of people living in poverty has increased, so have the number of Americans who have "made it" financially by the time they have reached midlife. They have worked so hard, often with two wage earners per household, that they have forgotten how to play. With this increased free time, some three hundred colleges now offer degree programs in "leisure studies"—teaching people how to relax so that they, in turn, can teach the big market out there how to use discretionary time after reaching financial security. This is not unique to America, of course, and it is true of the churched, the dechurched and the unchurched as well. The average mainline church member is undistinguishable from anyone else in society when it comes to living for profits, possessions and personal gain.

A recent study by "empty tomb, inc.," a non-profit research and service organization in Champaign, Illinois, with a grant from the Lilly Endowment, reports that Americans are wealthier and have far more disposable income today but are giving a smaller proportion of their income to their churches. The study, which covers a seventeen-year period, found that in 1968 Roman Catholics and Protestants from thirty-one denominations gave 3.05 percent of income after taxes to their churches. By 1985 that had dropped to 2.79 percent despite disproportionate gains in income. The same group spends 12 percent on leisure activities, billions on cut flowers, pets, lawns and microwave popcorn. A Gallup poll similarly revealed that donations to charity decrease as income increases. Brian O'Connell, president of the Independent Sector, a non-profit coalition of 650 corporate, volunteer and foundation organizations, said, "Giving and volunteering in America is a stark contrast between heart-warming generosity and bone-chilling selfishness." Most revealing was that members of low to moderate income families were more generous than their upper-income counterparts. O'Connell concluded, "Contrary to popular opinion, the well-to-do American cannot be described as generous." Are we suffering from compassion fatigue, or have we simply been victimized and enslaved by our own fortunes?

This behavior stands out in bold relief against Paul's remark to Timothy, "For loving money leads to all kinds of evil, and some men in the struggle to be rich have lost their faith and caused themselves untold agonies of mind" (1 Tim. 6:10 Phillips). Most of us cannot accept this part of the gospel. In the church, money and possessions are hushed subjects, not generally preached about, spoken of or dealt with in study or prayer groups. They are considered too personal, too private, because, as I said earlier, the subject of money touches our *sanctum sanctorum*—our true religion. Money and possessions are unapproachable topics for most preachers and other servants.

It is, furthermore, regarded as un-American to identify profits and possessions as obstacles to spiritual growth. In response to the minister who raises the subject, people often accuse, defensively, "All the minister ever talks about is money." It is easier, then, for a minister to be safe and job-secure and not mention money or generosity very often, except to say "thanks" for it.

A clergy colleague of mine is a remarkable exception to the general experience. He has recognized the centrality of stewardship and generosity in giving as the key to Christian discipleship. A bit sad, he told me that only at this late time in his ministry has he become bold enough to speak straightforwardly about money, generosity and holistic stewardship. As he gets closer to retirement and has fewer concerns about job and career, he feels freer to teach and speak without pulling punches. And he is surprised to find that for the most part his congregation is responding affirmatively to his challenges. I was inspired by his testimony, and I wished that others could find that courage at a younger age.

Jesus understood what the pursuit of possessions and profits do to the human spirit. Few things have a greater adverse effect upon the spiritual search of well-meaning seekers than abundance and affluence. Wealth paralyzes us; it is every bit as addictive as alcohol and drugs. To have a lasting love affair with materialism is to surrender the heart totally with room for no other love. As Thoreau wrote, "Most of the luxuries, and many of the so-called comforts, of life are not only not indispensable, but positive hindrances to the elevation of mankind."

It is important to remember one of the sources of the tragedy that befell Jesus and his community of disciples during the Week of the Passion: the betrayer Judas was beguiled by money. It was he who held the "money box" of the community (John 13:29), probably as the treasurer; and it was Judas who received bribe money from the chief priests (Mark 14:10–11). Judas may have had delusions of grandeur about the possibilities of an earthly king and about what money could buy. Money has a powerful mystique for most people. We have seen what this power has done to some televangelists and their money brokers. Profits and power have brought corruption and ruin to personal lives, to the business world, to government and to the institutions of religion.

Since we hear so few sermons and read so little about the "terrible truths" of Jesus, we can only help ourselves by reviewing some of them again. They are terrible truths for us because they impinge upon our profits and possessions; their message makes us uncomfortable. Twenty of the thirty-nine teaching parables of Jesus are directly related to stewardship and the use of and approach to gifts. Moreover, at many other points in his recorded ministry and teaching, Jesus discussed the subject of money and wealth in what Millard Fuller of Habitat for Humanity calls "the economics of Jesus." Some of the "terrible truths" follow.

1. "Do not lay up treasures on earth, . . . For where your treasure is, there will your heart be also." (Matt. 6:19–21)

2. "You cannot serve God and mammon." (Matt. 6:24/Luke 16:13)

3. "Therefore I tell you, do not be anxious about your life, what you shall eat or what you shall drink, nor about your body, what you shall put on. Is not life more than food, and the body more than clothing?" (Matt. 6:25)

4. "For whoever would save his life will lose it; and whoever loses his life for my sake and the gospel's will save it. For what

does it profit a man to gain the whole world and forfeit his life?" (Matt. 10:39/Mark 8:35–36/Luke 17:33/John 12:25)

5. "So therefore, whoever of you does not renounce all that he has cannot be my disciple." (Luke 14:33)

6. "Take heed and beware of all covetousness; for a man's life does not consist in the abundance of his possessions." (Luke 12:15)

7. The parable of the rich fool follows: "Fool, so is he who lays up treasure for himself, and is not rich toward God." (Luke 12:16–21)

8. "Sell your possessions, and give alms; provide yourselves with purses that do not grow old, with a treasure in the heavens that does not fail, where no thief approaches and no moth destroys. For where your treasure is, there will your heart be also." (Luke 12:33, 34)

9. The parable of the rich man and Lazarus: "But Abraham said, 'Son, remember that you in your lifetime received your good things, and Lazarus in like manner evil things; but now he is comforted here, and you are in anguish.'" (Luke 16:25)

10. The encounter with the rich young ruler: "One thing you lack. Sell all that you have and distribute it to the poor, and you will have treasure in heaven; and come follow me." (Luke 18:22/Mark 10:21/Matt. 19:21)

11. "How hard it is for those who have riches to enter the Kingdom of God! For it is easier for a camel to go through the eye of a needle than for a rich man to enter the Kingdom of God." (Luke 18:24–25)

12. "Remembering the words of the Lord Jesus, how he said, 'It is more blessed to give than to receive.'" (Acts 20:35, Paul quoting Jesus)

A MODEL CHURCH

In light of this "gloves-off" teaching of Jesus, it is instructive to look again at the formation and practice of the first Christian community as it is detailed in the Book of Acts.

This is the apostolic church of Peter, John and the rest of the faithful fellowship in the weeks following Christ's death and resurrection. The post-Pentecost church is described as a foretaste of the "peaceable kingdom"; nowhere is a more pure and idyllic community setting found in scripture.

The single, most significant identifying feature of this model community, the first New Testament church, is that it was formed around the relationship of its members to their personal goods and possessions. Yes, it *was* a religious commune, the first great communist experiment. If the church, in light of the freshly recalled teachings and practices of Jesus, was to be faithful to its mandate, then the first requirement of its adherents would be the stewarding of their gifts and possessions.

The blueprint of the model community is described by Luke:

> So those who received his word were baptized, and there were added that day about three thousand souls. And they devoted themselves to the apostles' teaching and fellowship, to the breaking of bread and the prayers. And fear came upon every soul; and many wonders and signs were done through the apostles. And all who believed were together and had all things in common; and they sold their possessions and goods and distributed them to all, as any had need. And day by day, attending the temple together and breaking bread in their homes, they partook of food with *glad and generous hearts,* praising God and having favor with all the people. And the Lord added to their number day by day those who were being saved. (Acts 2:41–47, my italics)

> Now the company of those who believed were of one heart and soul, and no one said that any of the things which he possessed was his own, but they had everything in common. And with great power the apostles gave their testimony to the resurrection of the Lord Jesus, and great grace was upon them all. There was not a needy person among them, for as many as were possessors of lands or houses sold them, and brought the

> proceeds of what was sold and laid it at the apostles' feet; and distribution was made to each as any had need. Thus Joseph, who was surnamed by the apostles Barnabas (which means Son of encouragement), a Levite, a native of Cyprus, sold a field which belonged to him, and brought the money and laid it at the apostles' feet. (Acts 4:32–37)

Here is a model for our stewardship! The outstanding characteristic of the people is that they lived together "with glad and generous hearts." This was the one characteristic lacking in the otherwise religious rich young ruler in Luke 18:18–23. What a breakthrough it would be if today we could know the meaning of living with glad and generous hearts. A conversion to generosity would be like the pearl of great price in the parable; when he found it, the merchant went and sold all that he had and bought it. Stewarding our possessions for God and others and living with thankful and generous hearts is at the very core of our religious quest.

But sadly these attitudes are lacking in the mainline church and in Christianity today. This raises two serious questions: Can Christian community and a capitalist materialistic system coexist? Can an affluent Christian church and an impoverished world of nations find common ground? Scott Libbey of the UCC Board for World Ministries quotes Bishop Ding of the Theological Seminary on Nan Jing, China: "Only a church that is without privilege can be a bearer of the Gospel."

Is the model community of Acts an ancient ideal to view abstractly or a living, dynamic form to emulate in new and creative ways?

THE AMERICAN CHURCH TODAY

We have a long way to go if we are to rediscover our mandate to live as stewards of gifts with glad and generous hearts. At least one indicator of the level of commitment to the Christian faith and life is the measure of support that confirmed members contribute financially to their church. The reports of at least one segment of mainline Protestantism indicate marginal, almost token, financial support of the church by most of its members. A brief example, which I believe to be reflective of many of the mainline churches, is the Wisconsin Conference of the United Church of Christ. This is a part of the church with which I have worked very closely for many years, and it is an excellent sample of the larger picture. Wisconsin is representative of mid-America, and it includes neither the higher income and higher cost of living areas of the two coasts, nor the lower income/lower cost areas of numerous other states.[1]

I use the term "per capita personal income" to mean the total personal income of all residents divided by the total resident population (every man, woman, child), excluding only those serving in the Armed Forces outside the country. The term "personal income" means income received by persons from all sources, that is, from participation in production, from transfer payments from government and business and from government interest, which is treated like a transfer payment. Personal income is the sum of private and government wage and salary disbursements, other labor income, farm and nonfarm properties income, rental income of persons, personal dividend income, personal interest income and transfer payments, minus personal contributions for social insurance. Personal income is measured before the deduction of personal income taxes and other personal taxes and is reported in current dollars. Thus, per capita personal income is the total personal income divided by the total resident state population.

The average total per capita personal income for all of the United States in the year 1988 was reported as $16,444 by the Department of Commerce. The State of Wisconsin runs fairly consistently at 90 to 100 percent of the national income average, thus representing a cross section of the nation. For 1988 the per capita personal income for every resident of Wisconsin was $15,444. Thus, for example, two persons living together had an average combined per capita income of $30,888 in 1988.

Meanwhile, in that same period, total membership of the Wisconsin Conference United Church of Christ was 76,514. Each member contributed, for all church purposes, a per capita gift of $256.67, which included offerings for the total local church expense, including capital expenses and the wider mission support. The wider mission portion, which is included in the $256.67, was $37.43 per member, or 72 cents per week. These figures represent an amount equal to 1.66 percent of annual personal income. Clearly, this is not faithful stewardship of gifts. Since it is generally representative of the mainline church picture, it is an important indicator and symptom of the poor health of American Protestantism.

Need we wonder why there is not greater spiritual depth among our churches and its members? By any standard of comparison, the people of Wisconsin as representative of America, have treasure, but since it is not invested in the church their hearts are not there either. The way of Jesus Christ and the message of the Gospel can have little global impact when practiced by a people who are so lacking in generosity and commitment. While most Americans today could live fairly well on a fraction of their income and have more disposable time than any other generation in history, the church languishes and retreats in the face of a world hungering and crying for the "good news."

The problem is clear. But there are no ready solutions. The greatest task the church faces now is to find ways to lead and teach people to turn away from insatiable self-service and toward service to others through living with thankful and generous hearts. An immediate but short-term approach is that if we must possess more and more, surely, at the minimum, we must also give more and more in the same measure. The church aside, discount it if you must, give self to others in significant and generous ways. It is the only path to spiritual discovery. Again, a voice from the Third World, Helder Camara, the Archbishop of Olinda and Recife, speaks of a bold generosity after the manner of the Son who was given:

> If you share your bread
> in fear,
> mistrustfully,
> undaringly,
> in a trice
> your bread
> will fail.
> Try sharing it
> without looking ahead,
> not thinking of the cost,
> unstintingly,
> like a son of the Lord
> of all the harvests in the world.[2]

8.

THE ABUSE
AND USE OF GIFTS

All you have shall someday be given;
Therefore give now, that the season of giving may be yours
And not your inheritors.
—Kahlil Gibran
On Giving, *The Prophet*

Humans were born, designed and created to be stewards, to be caretakers and tenders of whatever comes within the scope of their being in this life. In the 1930s pioneer environmentalist Aldo Leopold wrote that not only were humans a part of the earth community, they were the captains of the spaceship earth, yet another way of stating that humans are called to be stewards of creation. Where we do not carefully tend, manage and nurture the gifts within our grasp, things go awry; there is imbalance, inequity and unfairness—disaster. When humans fail to exercise their stewardship responsibility, world economies of goods become upset; the environment of our fragile earth is endangered; the depletion of resources becomes a threat.

77

THE ABUSE OF STEWARDSHIP

To understand stewardship is to know that it involves receiving as well as giving. To be the recipient of the gifts of God and creation, to receive them thankfully, and to know and to recognize the meaning of the gifts are all part of stewardship. One of our perennial problems, however, has been to understand correctly the part receiving plays in stewardship. Instead, the recipient often becomes swallowed up in the gifts; the gift of possessions becomes an end in itself. This deviant form of stewardship was described by Jesus in the parable of the rich fool (Luke 12:16–21) who knew only that more would be better. Instead of sharing his good fortune or investing it for the common good, he stored up more treasure for himself and was ungenerous toward God. Blind toward the giving side of stewardship, he died a very rich man; and for this, Jesus called him "fool."

HOARDING GIFTS

Educators and preachers of stewardship have long warned of the perils of prosperity and particularly of the tragedy, if not immorality, of dying rich in goods and property. Think of the irony of giving a lifetime to the gathering of possessions and then having your life summoned at roll call. Why do we try to live as if we will be here forever? No less than Andrew Carnegie said, "The man who dies rich dies disgraced." Some of the ultra-rich have understood this and practice stewardship more faithfully than the lesser-known wealthy. It is one matter, perhaps, to provide for one's closest family after years of common commitment, but another matter to enrich one's descendants. I have seen bumperstickers on cars that carry a distorted stewardship message, "We're spending our children's inheritance!" How much better it would be if they read, "We're giving away our estate." While it is true, as John Kenneth Galbraith wrote in his classic *Affluent Society*, that "public welfare has an extremely bad image in America," perhaps the merits of leaving this world naked in estate of personal possessions would have a profound effect on the First World's craze for acquisition. Suppose that upon death everyone's accumulated wealth, except basic provision for next of kin, were surrendered for the public good?

I suggest this because the problem is only going to worsen. Americans who began their employment years in the two decades following World War II are the richest people in history. By the close of this century they will begin leaving a vast sum of financial assets and property. The baby boomers stand to inherit this wealth. The Conference Board, a business-research organization in New York stated recently that people over 65, who account for 20 percent of all American households, hold 40 percent of the nation's personal financial assets. The board said, "Never before has a retiring generation been so well-heeled, and never before have so many been destined to inherit so much."[1] The sociologists and economists call this process "intergenerational wealth transfer," and they argue over the effect it will have on the nation's economy. We must also wonder about the perils of prosperity and excess, the impact of easy wealth upon the moral and spiritual climate of a people and upon the imperative for stewarding and sharing vast inherited wealth. A question for the elderly rich is clear: Will my legacy prove to be a blessing or a curse to my inheritors? Gifts beyond one's willingness or ability to steward pose an enormous hazard to personal and societal well-being.

A film that speaks to the point is the 1983 movie *Family*

Business. It is the story of the eventual death of a wealthy man and the monumental struggle between his four sons over the inheritance and estate. How many funerals have ministers experienced where the main focus was not grief over the deceased but the rising tensions between family members over terms of the estate settlement. Where money is concerned it commands and overshadows all other considerations.

Can you envision the life orientation of people who would never expect to inherit *or* to bequeath large estates? In ancient times, Job considered the prospect: "Naked I came from my mother's womb, and naked shall I return; the Lord gave, and the Lord has taken away; blessed be the name of the Lord" (Job 1:21–22). The rich fool in Jesus' story never gave this a thought; hence he was a fool.

The biblical word is clear. "As for the rich in this world, charge them not to be haughty, not to set their hopes on uncertain riches, but on God who richly furnishes us with everything to enjoy. They are to do good, to be rich in good deeds, liberal and generous, thus laying up for them-selves a good foundation for the future, so that they may take hold of the life which is life indeed" (1 Tim. 6:17–19). This message is directed at the vast majority of Americans and people of the First World. In his autobiography, *With Head and Heart,* Howard Thurman tells of a visit to Howard University by Miriam Slade, the Englishwoman who had given up her affluent life in Britain not only to become a disciple of Gandhi in India but also to join his ashram as a member of the family community of which he was the center. "The subject of her address to the assembly was, in itself, a bold, almost arrogant challenge, but not quite so: 'He who has more than he needs for efficient work is a thief.' The essential point was quite clear and convincing. There is no moral justification for having food and a surfeit of creature comforts at one's disposal while numberless people all over the world in every country are without the necessities to survive. . . . Hers was a quiet, undramatic delivery, but the intensity of her passion gathered us all into a single embrace, and for one timeless interval we were bound together with all the people of the earth."[2]

INACTION

Inaction is another aberrant form of stewardship practice. It is receiving and recognizing gifts, perhaps even affirming God as the Giver, but refusing to do anything at all with the gifts. Being a steward implies action after the likeness of the God of creation and life or after the model of Jesus Christ who, having many gifts, surrendered them all and became the servant of all humankind. In the parable of talents (Matt. 25:14–30) the one-talent servant played it safe, refusing to take risk, burying his talent in the ground until the master returned. In a sense, his error was not that he failed to yield an increase in the talent, but that he did not make the attempt to increase his gift. After the model of God's own stewardship in Jesus Christ, it would have been better to have risked and failed than not to have made the attempt.

Every human achievement and breakthrough for the betterment of the human condition has resulted from risking and investing God's gifts for a continuing new creation. It is true that results are never assured, but to focus on results is to miss the point of participating with God the Giver in employing the gifts for the ongoing work. A farmer plants in spring with no guarantee of a crop. The winds and temperatures, the variable rains, and the capriciousness of nature are all factors in his success or failure. The meaning, however, is in the planting. As T. S. Eliot said: "For us, there is only the trying. The rest is not our business."

TO GIVE AND GIVE AGAIN

EVIL STEWARDSHIP

It must be said, however, that neglecting or refusing to use gifts on behalf of creation is better than practicing the greatest abuse of stewardship—the misuse or diabolical use of gifts. Throughout history, war, slavery, oppression, injustice, and discrimination against others have resulted from the abuse of gifts, including power and personal profit.

War is a violent insult to stewardship. Its murderous destruction of life, military and civilian, is the absolute contradiction of God the Giver of gifts. About war's voracious appetite Napoleon Bonaparte said, "I can use up 25,000 men a month." Looking to reverse that trend through a new stewardship, Albert Einstein looked ahead to a future when "the pioneers of a warless world are the young men and women who refuse military service." Recently, a friend accompanied me to view a piece of sculpture entitled "The Moving Wall," on temporary display in a local park. It is a half-scale replica of Washington's Vietnam Veterans' Memorial, one of several touring the country. It was a sobering moment to see the names of the 58,000 dead men and women with an average age of just nineteen years. These spent young lives should be properly mourned and remembered by a nation's act of stewardship. But they did not so much give their lives as have them taken from them by their country in the always uncertain and almost always unworthy cause of war. Working for the abolition of war is an act of reverence for life, an ultimate expression of stewardship. Dwight Eisenhower's fearful warning about the military-industrial complex and its power, profits and corruption was a warning against anti-stewardship. The elimination of arms would be an example of dispossession, of giving-up, of stewarding for peace.

The desecration of human and natural resources for the development, production and deployment of nuclear weapons is a crucifixion of the concept of stewardship. It is the most glaring example of the failure of stewardship ever known to humankind. Robert R. Wilson, one of the designers of the A-bomb, related that many of the project scientists at first felt exhilaration over their success. They exulted, "It worked! We did it!" But in the days and weeks following, they began to experience actual sickness and depression, which was followed by yet another reaction—a commitment to "never again." Robert Oppenheimer, head of the project, quoted a Hindu proverb after observing the extent of the first test blast: "I am become death, a destroyer of worlds." Renouncing the bomb and nuclear weapons development, Oppenheimer told a Harvard audience that the nuclear scientists have "known sin"; he soon lost his security clearance with the government and suffered humiliation and an early death.

I recall an evening in the early 1950s at McCormick Theological Seminary in Chicago. In a chapel filled to capacity, Harold C. Urey, Nobel Laureate in chemistry from the University of Chicago and one of the bomb's architects, spoke compellingly to the young theological students and faculty about the evils of nuclear weapons. While I do not believe he ever used the term "stewardship," it certainly was his subject, as he decried the misuse of the gifts of science and technology for destructive and barbaric purposes. And where will this rape of our own gifts and resources end?

The facts and statistics concerning the vast West/East capacity for mega-death and fifteen times overkill of everyone on earth do not need more than a mention here. Now we learn that even an underdeveloped nation like Pakistan has acquired the capability to produce fissionable material to be used in the construction of a nuclear weapon. At least seven nations now have that capability, while at least forty have nuclear potential. More than the cost and the misuse of money involved in weapons development, the misappropriation of gifts and resources, this profound symbol of death and annihilation is anti-God the Giver.

Compare the church world mission of the nineteenth century to the military world mission of the twentieth. The church mission was often suspect and questioned, in that the missionary movement was accompanied by economic and imperialistic exploitation. In comparison, though, the monstrous enterprise of today's military mission to arm those same countries should stagger our conscience. In the mutual West/East militarization of smaller nations, we downplay the merchanting of conventional weapons, forgetting that they are also capable of causing mass suffering and destruction. Perhaps, then, in terms of stewardship, it would be better to bury our gifts in the ground and await the return of the Master and God's wrath then to employ our talents for the purposes of darkness and death.

WHEN LIGHT BECOMES DARKNESS

Jesus addresses the abuse of gifts, that is, stewardship in reverse, by comparing and contrasting darkness and light. Light is a gift, since in creation God the Giver said, "'Let there be light'; and there was light" (Gen. 1:3). In the Sermon on the Mount, Jesus says, "You are the light of the world. . . . Let your light so shine before men that they may see your good works" (Matt. 5:14–16). In Jesus' biblical metaphor, darkness is evil, and it is expected to be evil. Its nature is to be evil since it is against God. But what if your good is turned into evil; what if your light is turned into darkness and becomes a corruption of stewardship? Then, more than a nonsteward, the creature caretaker becomes an anti-steward, a total rejection of God's intention for humanity.

In the Sermon on the Mount, Jesus likens the eye to the lamp of the body: if the eye is sound, the body will be filled with light. The light is to shine with good works. However, if the eye is not sound, but evil, the whole body will be filled with darkness. Then he describes the condition of reverse or alien stewardship: "If, then, the light in you is darkness, how great is the darkness" (Matt. 6:23). From darkness we expect nothing but darkness. We are shocked when the gifts of light become darkness; it is like walking from bright sunlight into a very dark place—utter blackness. Thoreau had this in mind undoubtedly when he wrote in *Walden*, "There is no odor so bad as that which arises from goodness tainted." Gifts of light transmogrified for the purposes of evil degrade stewardship.

It is interesting to note that Matt. 6:23 is found between the two great teachings on stewardship. Preceding it in vv. 19–21 is the laying-up-of-treasure passage; following is the instruction that one cannot serve God and mammon (v. 24). Clearly, central to the teaching of Jesus is the inclination toward the stewardship of gifts.

Illustrating the image of light becoming darkness, Howard Thurman, in his book *The Growing Edge*, portrays the minister who bears much light on the subject of religion.

> I am a minister; again and again I am impressed with the fact that it is not easy to grow in sympathy and understanding of other people. It is very easy to become professionally a religious person, professionally a minister, and let my knowledge of the Bible, my knowledge of the history of the Church, my knowledge of the psychology of religion, become a substitute for getting on my knees, seeking forgiveness of my sins, wrestling with my spirit in the presence of God. If I let my knowledge become a substitute for my understanding, then

the light that is in me becomes darkness. If the light that is in
me becomes darkness, what a darkness.[3]

The nuclear physicist, the teacher, the engineer, the physician, the steward of light-gifts in every person is vulnerable to abuse of their knowledge-gifts for the purposes of darkness and against the understanding of stewardship. When good gifts are turned into evil, the result overwhelms the heart and numbs the mind.

When our vast financial resources are turned toward the purposes of war, they disappear as military costs rise from millions, to billions, to trillions of dollars. How can we fathom the numbers? Recently Charles Lockyear, the treasurer and director of finance of the United Church of Christ, retired after twenty-seven years at the post. Lockyear noted that since 1962 slightly more than 500 million dollars had come through his office from the churches and conferences for basic support of the wider mission. I thought about that 500 million dollars, given over a twenty-seven year period by 6300 local congregations and just under 2 million members. All of those gifts, from all of those people, for all of those years—and yet the 500 million would barely cover the cost of one American Stealth bomber, 1989 version. Is it possible to justify the enormity of so much light turned to so much darkness?

We have gifts far beyond our moral grasp, gifts that have outrun our capacity to steward. The World Health Organization testifies that sanitary water is one of the earth's greatest problems and that most disease in Third World countries is related to impure water. By suspending international arms production for a matter of hours, enough money could be saved to provide clean water for every human on earth. As world population soared to more than 5 billion in mid-1988, the U.S. government sharply cut back its assistance to developing nations in the areas of family planning and birth control. Meanwhile, in a steward's nightmare, the military budget for offensive weapons of war swelled beyond belief. We have gifts and light that we do not understand and that turn on us and become our dark enemy.

CREATIVE STEWARDSHIP

Where does our corruption of gifts stop? We need to find ways to manage gifts that will work against the darkness. After all, the steward is called to be "the light of the world," to expose the works of darkness. Attempts to reverse the arms race and to change the climate of weapons frenzy are options open to all faithful stewards. As the super powers begin to take arms control more seriously, an unthinkable notion in the early 1980s, we must believe that the witness and protest of the church and many other peace-loving organizations has had an impact on their actions.

We can rejoice in the U.S./Soviet nuclear arms negotiations, which represent a move toward a more steward-worthy stance of openness, accord and handclasps. Designing, possessing and deploying weapons is, after all, incompatible with any understanding of stewardship. The gift of compromise is at the heart of all conflict resolution. Negotiation, with its give and take, its exploration of alternatives, its highlighting of common interests is by its very process the practice of stewardship. The wise manager, the faithful creature caretaker is by definition a negotiator who recognizes that a world without nuclear arms threatens no one and benefits all Roger Fisher and William Urey's fine book, *Getting to Yes* is a steward's handbook for the caretaking of resources and relationships.[4]

Even some fanciful approaches may be worth considering. What if nations shared all weapons technology and national security secrets by throwing open their files and strategies? What if all nuclear testing and research took place only on soil and within the bounds of the opponent's country? Could there be annual one-year exchanges of students, including teachers, by the millions, to facilitate cultural understanding, but also to curtail the possibility of attack upon one's own kin? The costs and logistics of such ventures would be far less than what is now spent on the development, production and deployment of weapons.

It is important that in stewarding creation and its gifts we employ our greatest gifts and shine our light on creative alternatives to the present drift toward global murder-suicide. In his great pastoral prayer, Paul Tillich ends with these intercessions:

> Prevent us from turning Thy gifts into causes of injury and self-destruction. Let a grateful mind protect us against national and personal disintegration. Turn us to Thee, the Source of our being, Eternal God! Amen.[5]

The job of the peacemaker is:

> To stop war
> To purify the world
> To get it saved from poverty and riches
> To heal the sick
> To comfort the sad
> To wake up those who have not found God
> To create joy and beauty wherever you go
> To find God in everything and in everyone.[6]

9.

GIFTS ARE NOT OUR OWN

A true Christian is a person who never for a moment forgets what God has done for him in Christ, and whose whole comportment and whole activity have their root in the sentiment of gratitude.

—John Baillie

UNEARNED GIFTS AND OBLIGATIONS

A friend working in the field of atmospheric research was a frequent traveler to Ascension Island in the south Atlantic Ocean. He tells of still-existing stands of Norfolk Pine trees, tall and straight, that were planted as seedlings by early whalers. They were to become a future source of masts for whaling ships damaged in storms. These trees clearly could never have benefited those early whalers, since the pines required years of growth before they would be usable as masts. They were planted by the whalers as an investment in the future, for others beyond themselves.

Every day we stand in the shade of trees we did not plant. We live in houses we did not build. We eat food we did not produce. We ponder ideas that are not original to us. So, too, we live a life in a body and with a mind and a spirit that we did not choose or create: Our birth was an event entirely apart from our consent or approval, wholly unmerited and unearned. We ponder the unique gift of each person, all of the incredible contributions that combine in the making of and providing for one individual human. Aren't we, as creature caretakers, obliged to contribute to life in the same manner in which we have received from God, from creation, from others? The biblical mandate of Jesus to the disciples, as he sent them out with the gospel, is focused for us here, "Give as you have received, without any charge whatever" (Matt. 10:8 Phillips), or in the time-honored succinct King James translation, "Freely ye have received, freely give."

To be continually on the receiving end of life and never feel obliged to contribute is avaricious and self-indulgent. It is like the person who does not eat, simply and thankfully, for nourishment and satisfaction, but who practices gluttony, not appreciating or savoring the food. We have only to observe the way in which Americans celebrate Thanksgiving Day as a special day of the year created to express thankfulness. Albeit a secular holiday with some religious overtones, there is little about it that reflects genuine thankful hearts. It is, moreover, often just another opportunity to set a table with more dishes than it is possible to taste or experience. It is a time to be the gourmand, to gorge oneself with one more serving or just another piece or slice. True, the Pilgrims celebrated the first Thanksgiving, which included a feast, but is there that same kind of thankfulness in our celebration today? The way in which we observe Thanksgiving is a metaphor for our opulent and over-prosperous lives. It is the rejection of the practice of stewardship. What if Thanksgiving Day meant a time for prayer, fasting and giving an extravagant gift to a charitable cause as a symbol of living with a thankful and generous heart? Then, could there be such a Thanksgiving Day every week?

In *Deep Is the Hunger,* a special book that has become a tutor of my own spirit, Howard Thurman writes of our indebtedness to life that is given so that we might live:

> To be alive is to participate responsibly in the experiences of life. We say grace at meat not only because we feel a sense of gratitude to God for sustaining providence, but out of a sense of responsibility to the life that has been yielded in order that we may be sustained for one more day. The bacon that a person ate for breakfast, at some moment in the past, was alive and vibrant with an elemental health and vigor. Who can measure the reaches of aliveness of a hog, wallowing in murky contentment in the summer sun? There comes a day when he must die—"be slaughtered" is the acrid word we use. What are the paroxysms of lightening intimations of meanings that thud through his body at the first fall of the bludgeon? In utter accuracy, he dies that we may live. Thus, as we partake of his body, we pause, like the stillness of absolute motion, to salute his leave-taking of life. Because of what he yielded and because of the myriad yieldings of many forms of life, we are able to live and carry on. This means that our life is not our own. Every minute of life, we are faced with the relentless urgency to make good in our own lives for the lives that are lost for us.[1]

Thurman raises here the issue of what we owe to life for the gift of life and the gifts in life that we have received. The least we owe is to respond to every situation and opportunity before us with a generous and a thankful heart. We owe a response to persons and circumstances, even difficult ones, of openness, creativity and positivity. We must make our treasure of gifts vulnerable, our smiles, our embraces, our ideas and insights, our time and attention, our resources of skills, abilities and possessions. A former college professor of mine offered a special insight that has stayed with me over the years. How does one respond to this kind of grace or free gift? To live with integrity, we must recognize that we are under a profound

TO GIVE AND GIVE AGAIN

obligation to release that gift, to share the insight with
other searchers, to live up to its meanings and imperatives
as long as we breathe. To hold it fast or to hide it or to
clutch it within the stronghold of the self is to become a
miser, a noncontributor and a failed steward. Life has a
claim upon our gifts, most of which we neither earned nor
deserved. But they came, and our only ethical response
can be to yield in kind with a thankful and generous heart.

SELF-SATISFACTION AND GENEROSITY

One of the most vexing responses to personal profit and
prosperity is the common attitude, "I've gotten where I am
and have accumulated my gains through sweat, sacrifice
and hard work. If a lot of the people I see or hear about
would labor as hard as I have, they wouldn't be poor and
on welfare." Who gave this arrogant person the strength of
body, the mental prowess, the inherited favored cultural
setting, perhaps the racial advantage and the good fortune
to make prosperity possible? They were all gifts of grace,
unmerited windfalls, favors of creation. Too often, life is
regarded as a reward to be won rather than a gift to be
received. Most of us have received returns without investment. We have reaped where we have never sown. But we
must remember that nothing is ours to keep; it is ours only
to give and share, for sooner or later comes the summons
to death, and then the question that Jesus asked of the rich
fool, "The things you have prepared, whose will they be?"
(Luke 12:20b). The grasping hand, the clenched fist, the
hardened heart are all rejections of stewardship.

In a real sense, all argument for stewardship is invalid,
apart from the hearer's conviction that all we have and all
we are is a gift from God. As long as there is a holdout for
the conviction that we have gained or achieved our lives by
ourselves, there is no room for the concept of stewardship.

The question, What do I owe to life for the gift and the gifts of life that I have received? makes no sense while I insist that I have attained my own gifts and earned my own way. Deuteronomy 8 denies this attitude, again and again affirming the source of Israel's abundant blessings and concluding by warning, "Beware lest you say in your heart, 'My power and the might of my hand have gotten me this wealth.' You shall remember the Lord your God, for it is he who gives you the power to get wealth" (Deut. 8:17–18). Stewardship has a chance if God is acknowledged as the Giver, for then the heart will become vulnerable to generosity.

We must become conscious of the gifts of opportunity that are ours because people, known and unknown, opened doors for us. Think of our heritage, how we live by the fruits of the labors of countless generations who lived before us and without whom our own lives would have little meaning. Ideas, books, handclasps, a word of encouragement at the right moment, someone's courageous act, the genius of a disciplined scientist or artist, the sudden presence of some "stranger in the night" at our point of most immediate need are all the gift of "angels unawares." In this sentiment, John Donne wrote, "No man is an island, entire of itself; every man is a piece of the continent, a part of the main . . . any man's death diminishes me, because I am involved in mankind." A well-lived life is a shared process of mutual giving and receiving, life dependent upon life through deep interconnections and interdependence.

Howard Thurman, in his *Meditations of the Heart,* tells the story of a very ordinary, anonymous man who was walking along a sidewalk at the close of day. Near the curbstone, a group of birds was pecking away, trying to open a pink paper bag. They seemed to be quarreling as they pecked. There must have been many suggestions about the best way to get at the crumbs inside. The man walked over to the spot and the birds took flight, settling at a respectful distance, watching. With his foot, he turned the bag over, examined it with care, and then emptied the bag of its contents of bread crumbs. When he had done this, he resumed his walk with never a backward glance. As soon as he disappeared, the birds returned to find that a miracle had taken place. Instead of a tightly closed bag, there was before them a full abundance for satisfying their needs.

Any careful scrutiny of our own lives reveals that we have been in the birds' predicament again and again. Some great need of our life may have stopped us or blocked us, but then an unexpected stranger or unknown writer, or a comment from a friend triggered a miracle. Thurman concludes, "However self-sufficient we are, our strength is always being supplied by others unknown to us whose paths led them down our street or by our house at the moment that we needed the light they could give us. We are, all of us, the birds and we are, all of us, the man."[2] There is a time to receive and a time to give in the stewarding of the gifts of creation.

THE STEWARDSHIP OF TIME

There is also the gift of time—how do we caretake it, invest it and spend it? Studies and seminars in "time management" are really exercises in the stewardship of time. Every day, in our habits and practices in the use of time, we undermine whatever possibility there is for spiritual discovery and healthy interpersonal relationships. Perhaps thinking of misused or unstewarded time, Thoreau wrote, "As if you could kill time without injuring eternity." Always in a rush and frenzied, we leave little time for experiencing and absorbing the meaning of the moment. For most of us, life is a matter of what happens while we are making other plans. The stewarding of hours and days is dramatized and legalized for us in the Fourth Commandment. Of the seven-day week, six days are to be given to commerce and work, but by divine decree the seventh day is to be different, a holy day of rest, a sabbath, a convocation of the community. This is a clear call to the caretaking of time.

I learned of the principle of being attentive to the moment at hand at a retreat with the Capuchin Brothers. They spoke of the book *Miracle of Mindfulness* by the Asian teacher Thich Nhat Hanh, who suggested a stewardship of time that comes from being present to each moment given to us as a gift. The point was illustrated by the story of a pilgrim on retreat who wanted to be helpful by doing some routine task. He asked about whether he could assist in doing the dishes after meals. The Abbot said no, explaining that most people do the dishes so that they can be done doing the dishes. What is needed instead, he said is that one do the dishes in order to do the dishes, that is, to be mindful of the task, to feel the squeak of the towel against the hot wetness of the plate, to enjoy the sparkle and shine, to be aware of the present experience. Otherwise, it is like walking through a redwood forest and ignoring its beauty while making plans for the next meal, or designing the agenda for tomorrow's meeting. Similarly, we often are thinking of our response while another is speaking to us; we hear without listening. At meal time, especially with fast foods, we eat without savoring.

Stewardship is lingering over a meal that has been thoughtfully prepared and receiving the fellowship of the company with whom we celebrate the gift. Frequently we are figuratively somewhere other than where we are.

When this becomes a pattern, we become aliens in our own environment. We must actively practice mindfulness and *be there* for ourselves and, in turn, others.

We did not create our own time. Our days, hours and minutes are a gift, given to us as caretakers for use in the ongoing work of creation and redemption. I recall Martin Luther King, Jr., speaking to the urgency of this task, concluded a sermon at the Chicago Sunday Evening Club with these lines, which I saved:

> A tiny little minute, just sixty seconds in it,
> I didn't choose it,
> I can't abuse it,
> It's up to me to use it,
> A tiny little minute, just sixty seconds in it,
> But eternity, eternity, eternity is in it.

Because of our human limitations of time and resources we cannot do everything. But as freely as we have received, so freely we must give, that our lives may be not one-sided or top-heavy with abundance, but whole and complete as we contribute by casting our seed upon the wind, our bread upon the waters and our moments to redemptive tasks.

10.

OURS
FOR THE TAKING

As long as the light lasts
the going will be easy . . .
Once the light fails
remember
that you can turn yourself
into a blazing torch
able to light up
pitch-black paths
and the most tortuous mazes.[1]
—Dom Helder Camara

LIVING OUT OF THE SELF

D.T. Niles, post-World War II Third World church person and theologian, was gifted with many insights that still ring with truth. One of these is, "Mission is to the church as fire is to burning." If you extinguish the flame, the burning ceases. If the church puts aside mission to others, it loses its meaning. Many congregations still regard mission as an option to ministry, as something they should do or at least might do. Rare is the congregation that exists for

97

mission and whose reason for being is for others beyond itself. Often mission is regarded as ministry *within* our own community of faith, that is, supporting each other's needs and encouraging the faith of others. This is a limited sense of mission indeed. And it is relatively easy to satisfy this mission.

Congregations, however prosperous, that live unto themselves betray Jesus' mandate and are not the stewards of gifts from God the Giver. No institution other than the church exists for giving itself away for others. That is the unique mark of the church. Congregations must be models for their members in the imitation of Christ. A congregation models stewardship by its faithfulness to mission. All too often congregations mirror their members' natural selves, which means in our culture, people captive to the pursuit of profits and possessions. Churches' values are reflected in such banalities as, "Look out for numero uno," or "Charity begins at home." How can individuals be expected to embrace a life of stewarding God's gifts if that life is not modeled in and by congregations?

Ordained ministers are generally positive models of stewardship. I found this to be true in an informal and anonymous survey I conducted three years ago among clergy of part of the Wisconsin Conference, UCC. I asked them what they had contributed financially to the church that year. The results were beyond anything I would have guessed; the average contribution was $1,338, more than $25 per week—and this from families or single people whose average income would be just above the average for Wisconsin's personal per capita income. This is far above the average gift of corresponding lay persons. And perhaps this is how it should be. But while most ministers will be found among the most generous of contributors to the church and community, they are reticent about revealing their personal giving patterns, reflecting society's "religious" secrecy about anything pertaining to money or possessions. Lay people are often surprised to learn that their pastors give to the church at all and that they pay taxes. Perhaps they should share their patterns of giving with others, in openness and witnessing, and thereby play a role in stewardship education. For lifestyle and in faithful steward role modeling—in contrast to the electronic entertainment ministers—most Protestant clergy are excellent examples of generous giving.

Churches themselves must be asked, How big is the world in which you live? Is your world only as big as yourself or your family? Is your church's world only as high as the steeple and as wide as the parking lot? Gordon Allport, after discussing the components of personal mental health and well-being, poses the question, "Can one be truly sound in mind unless one takes upon himself some of the redemptive tasks in the world today?" Whole people can not exist in the midst of a broken world. He continues, "In theological terms, the extrinsically religious person turns to God, but does not turn away from self. Intrinsic religion is a hunger for, and a commitment to, an ideal unification of one's life, but always under a unifying concept of the nature of all existence."[2] This affirms the practice of stewardship at its very essence.

TAKE YOUR SHARE

If stewardship is giving in imitation of Christ, as I have noted, it is also receiving and taking. In 2 Timothy, Paul offers two exhortations to *taking* that are instructive to the steward. First he says, "But take your share of suffering for the Gospel in the power of God" (2 Tim. 1:8b); he continues, "Take your share of suffering as a good soldier of Christ Jesus" (2 Tim. 2:3). As Americans, we have taken and received a vast abundance of wealth and possessions while surrounded by a world of indescribable misery and pain.

Having taken more than our share of the earth's abundance, we need also to take our share of privation through bearing the burdens of others. What is ours for the taking? "If anyone would be my disciple, let him deny himself and *take* up his cross, and follow me." This is the stewardship model of taking, in which we accept for ourselves some of the redemptive tasks of the world around us. Unless we take on our share of the world's suffering and misery, we cannot survive as a nation, we cannot, as a church, be counted as stewards of God's gifts. Mission through the stewarding of our gifts on behalf of others is the only way the church can stay vital and the only way we can attain spiritual awakening.

James Forbes, Jr., minister of Riverside Church in New York City, has said,

> The community that I came up in had the understanding that if God blessed you, you at least ought to have the common decency to invest in some things that God is concerned about. That meant you would sacrifice. You would pay your tithes. When you got special blessings, you would make a special offering. It became natural.
>
> I believe that the culture in which we find ourselves has to learn that lesson. It has to be taught that it is actually demonic to receive without investing with some sense of reciprocity. . . . When I have been able to discover how fragile the threads of life are, when I discover the foundations on which I stand in times when everything begins to fall away around me, when I discover how dependent I am upon God, it seems natural to me to ask what I can render unto the Lord for all God's benefits to me? I'm just beginning to discern that hoarding resources may give temporary satisfaction and delight; but the long-term consequence is the necessity to secure myself against those who feel defrauded by my hoarding of the resources of the good earth.[3]

THE SAINT AS MODEL

When I look for models of the giving of self through the taking on of redemptive tasks, I turn to the saints, official and unofficial, of the church and the world. A saint has been defined as one in whom Christ is seen to live again. Certainly the *imitatio Christi* to which we are all called is a good definition. Saints model several common characteristics, although their work and styles can vary widely. The first characteristic after the model and teaching of Jesus usually involves voluntary poverty, ultimate stewardship. Many saints experienced lives of early privilege so that true saintliness would seem synonymous with dispossession. On the subject of wealth, Albert Einstein wrote, "Money only appeals to selfishness and always tempts its owners irresistibly to abuse it. Can anyone imagine Moses, Jesus or Gandhi armed with the moneybags of Carnegie?"[4] Other shared traits of the saints are service, charity, loving kindness and a life totally oriented to others rather than self.

Perhaps the most common attribute shared by the saints is their taking upon themselves some of the redemptive tasks of the world around them. By so stewarding the gift and gifts of their lives, they reach a state that I think of as total charity, complete selflessness. The word "charity" is translated as "love" in 1 Corinthians 13 (KJV). But as charity, love is linked to action, to benevolence, so the Latin root *caritas* means "active love." The use of the word "charity" in 1 Corinthians 13 will not permit us to understand love as an abstract principle, because charity is something one "does" or "becomes." There are three levels of "love in action," or charity. The least level is "giving." "Doing" is another level of charity but is behavior that still falls short of saintliness. A saint reaches the ultimate level of the stewardship of charity, that of "being" in a complete state of self-surrender. Being in the condition of self-lessness for others, in imitation of Christ, the saint becomes redemptive, his or her life an incarnate sacrament.

There is a host of model stewards, known and unknown, saints and martyrs: Augustine, Benedict, Boniface, Elizabeth of Marburg, Joan of Arc, from centuries past. From the present, Leo Tolstoy, Mahatma Gandhi, Jane Addams, Albert Schweitzer, Martin Luther King, Jr., Mother Teresa and the numberless lesser saints cherished by each of us, all of them living a style of complete charity, including giving, doing and being after the model of Jesus' call to stewardship: "For whoever would save his life will lose it, and whoever loses his life for my sake will find it" (Matt. 16:25).

Thus, could Francis of Assisi pray, "Help me to learn that in giving, I may receive; in forgetting self, I may find life eternal." His life and his way, after an over-privileged youth, were marked by a profound sense of stewardship, the giving away of the gift of life itself in thankful generosity to others and to the creatures of nature and creation. From any serious reading of lives which became holy, it is clear that right relations with self, with neighbor and with God are possible only as we come to terms with the stewardship of gifts and possessions.

Three contemporaries of the twentieth century, all Nobel Prize laureates for peace, amplify the centrality of charity to the saintly life. Well-known to millions of all faiths, and to millions of others beyond creeds, nationalities or race, are Albert Schweitzer, Mother Teresa and Martin Luther King, Jr., three servants of humanity who are foremost among those celebrated for the practice of stewardship in this century. Each supremely gifted in a variety of ways, all chose to pour out themselves in great generosity in behalf of universal causes of compassion, justice and mercy. In the definition and practice of stewardship, it would be difficult to improve on the examples of these three as contemporary models for churches, for society and for all creature caretakers.

ALBERT SCHWEITZER

Born in 1875 and reared in comfortable Gunsbach in the Alsace Lorraine, Albert Schweitzer, the son of a Lutheran pastor, was gifted and multitalented. He studied theology in Strasbourg with great distinction. His genius in music and organ led to study with Charles Maria Widor in Paris. In the careful stewarding of his years, he resolved to live until the age of thirty for science and art, but thereafter to give his life "to the direct service of humankind." Years later, after visiting Schweitzer at the compound on the Ogowe River, Norman Cousins quotes him reflecting on his own life.

> As a young man, my main ambition was to be a good minister. I completed my studies; then, after a while I started to teach. I became the principal of the seminary (in Strasbourg). All this while, I had been studying and thinking about the life of Jesus and the meaning of Jesus. And the more I studied and thought, the more convinced I became that Christian theology had become over-complicated.
>
> I decided I would leave the seminary. Instead of trying to get acceptance for my ideas, involving painful controversy, I decided I would make my life my argument. I would advocate the things I believed, in terms of the life I lived and what I did. Instead of vocalizing my belief in the existence of God within each of us, I would attempt to have my life and work say what I believed.[5]

So one of the most brilliant interpreters of the organ compositions of J.S. Bach, a philosopher/theologian of highest distinction abandoned careers in those fields to study medicine and establish a jungle hospital in Africa. This became his life statement, the stewardship of his life. Of his world view, Schweitzer wrote,

> I could not but feel with a sympathy full of regret all the pain that I saw around me, not only that of men but that of the whole creation. From this community of suffering I have never tried to withdraw myself. It seemed to me a matter of course that we should all take our share of the burden of pain which lies upon the world.[6]

A cornerstone for understanding stewardship is Albert Schweitzer's life- and gift-affirming principle, his ethic of "reverence for life." It sustained him throughout his own life, and he offered what the principle could do for every person.

> Reverence for life . . . forces him without cessation to be concerned with all other human destinies which are going through their life course around him, and to give himself as a man to the man who needs a fellowman. It does not allow the scholar to live with his science alone, even if it is very useful to the community in so doing. It does not permit the artist to exist only for his art, even if he gives inspiration to many by its means. It refuses to let the business man imagine that he fulfills all legitimate demands in the course of his business activities. It demands from all that they should sacrifice a portion of their own lives for others.[7]

Reverence for life is a dynamic principle that if acted upon results in a faithful stewardship. All of creation becomes a gift to be nurtured and sustained. Days and hours themselves take on new meaning, received as grace, to be not squandered but cherished and spent generously, including others with a thankful heart. Possessions and goods are not greedily accumulated but thankfully received, in whatever portion, and then shared in reverence and service for all humankind.

MOTHER TERESA

She was born of a wealthy, comfortable, happy family in Albania and, until age thirty-eight, was a teaching nun. While on a retreat, Mother Teresa received a "call" to abandon everything and go to work among the poorest of the poor in the slums of Calcutta in Bengal, India. Here, in a ministry to the hopeless and the dying, she became the "angel of Calcutta" with her band of sisters dressed in white and blue. Her Roman Catholic order began in 1948 and is called Missionaries of Charity.

Giving love-charity and generosity is the heart of the order. Mother Teresa insists that the sisters teach not through words but through their actions and smiles. When she visited America several years ago, Mother Teresa observed, "Your 'muchness' is suffocating," noting that both poverty and affluence are failures of stewardship.

Of the growing work of the Missionaries of Charity, she says, "We preach Christ without preaching. Not by words, but by putting his love and our love into a living action of serving the people in their needs; by loving and serving the dying, the homeless, the abandoned destitute, the lepers." Mother Teresa has written very little and speaks only briefly and infrequently. To correspondents she says, "Don't become offended if you do not receive an answer: our work is really big and we do not have time left to write letters." One day a contributor to the mission was told, "I hope you are not giving only your surplus. You must give what costs you, make a sacrifice, go without something you like, that your gift may have value before God. Then you will be truly brothers and sisters to the poor who are deprived of even the things they need."[8]

TO GIVE AND GIVE AGAIN

MARTIN LUTHER KING, JR.

How privileged we have been to live in an age when the life and spirit of Martin Luther King, Jr., was present among us. He was the apostle of racial justice, its centering love force and the focusing point for the brotherhood and sisterhood of all humans. We are moved and directed today by his great struggle in the 1950s and 1960s, by the effects of the stewarding of his great gifts for the cause of human freedom and by the sacrifice of his very life that one day all may say, "Free at last, free at last. Thank God Almighty, I'm free at last."

A quote from King will suffice to illuminate the fact that not only did he preach and teach the necessity of stewarding self-sacrifice to any life of meaning but he was himself a supreme steward, laying down his life for his cause, his friends and the continuing work of creation.

> No man has learned to live until he can rise above the narrow confines of his individualistic concerns to the broader concerns of all humanity. Length without breadth is like a self-contained tributary having no outward flow to the ocean. Stagnant, still and stale, it lacks both life and freshness. In order to live creatively and meaningfully, our self-concern must be wedded to the other-concern.[9]

SUMMARY

All too familiar with receiving and taking the gifts of life, the creature caretaker is called to a new meaning of taking, a meaning not desired or understood by most Americans. It is the taking upon ourselves of some of the many redemptive tasks in the world. And the give and take is not done according to the archaic stewardship principle of "eye for eye, tooth for tooth but according to a stewardship recast in the economics of Jesus' statement, "But I say to you!" It is the stewardship of "taking upon oneself" by generously giving oneself. It is found in the remark, "Give to the man who asks anything of you, and don't turn away from the man who wants to borrow" (Matt. 5:42 Phillips).

This is the spirit of the new creation which beckons for our participation in its coming. It calls to us from the pastoral letter: "Serve one another with the particular gifts God has given each of you, as faithful dispensers [stewards] of the wonderful varied grace of God" (1 Pet. 4:10 Phillips). We do not always know what the new creation in Christ means, but of this we can be certain: somehow it hangs together through the way in which we relate to all other life in the stewardship of our gifts and possessions. We look to the saints for the surest clue.

11.

GIVING WITHOUT COUNTING

Awake, Awake to Love and Work
To give and give, and give again, what God hath given thee;
To spend thyself nor count the cost; to serve right gloriously
The God who gave all worlds that are, and all that are to be.[1]
—G. A. Studdert-Kennedy

If Jesus had calculated the cost of his commitment, if he had measured the dregs of the bitter cup that he drank, he might have let his own will prevail. But, not counting the cost, he emptied himself of divine privilege, scorning human opportunity and gain, and humbled himself as a servant of all. This is the ultimate pattern of giving, which looms as a glorious example to all who would be followers of Jesus Christ and to which saints have aspired across the centuries. In Jesus' gift of himself, we have been bought at a great and costly price. The gift requires a response.

STEWARDSHIP AND RIGHT RELATIONS

While our salvation in Christ has been accomplished, how does the person of faith determine the bounds of

108

responsibility in keeping good faith with God's gifts? This is a question from the ages. Standing among the excavated ruins at Samaria-Sebaste in northern Israel recently, I thought of the social and economic injustices that scandalized both Israel and Judah in the eighth century B.C. Around these ruins, Ahab and Jezebel robbed Naboth of his vineyard and land and caused Elijah to condemn their act of unlawful possession.

As Jesus favored the poor, so the prophets cared about human issues, writing as much about economics and earthly realities such as wealth and poverty as they did about religious practices and relations to God. Indeed, they saw the stewardship of goods and property, as did Jesus, as the means of a proper relationship with God and neighbor.

In 722–21 B.C., Samaria was captured and destroyed by the Assyrians. To the south in Judah the prophet Micah was warning the people against the same fate befalling them. He set the standard for a proper response of thankfulness for God's gifts by asking, "With what shall I come before the Lord, and bow myself before God on high?" (Mic. 6:6a). Micah preceded his question by rehearsing the acts and gifts of God: deliverance from Egypt, servant gifts in the persons of Moses, Aaron, Miriam, the saving acts of God for his people. The prophet answered it by an initial review of a programmed list of inappropriate formulas for giving in response to God's gifts. True gifts are not characterized by some measured schedule. "Shall I come before him with burnt offerings, with calves a year old? Will the Lord be pleased with thousands of rams, or ten thousands of rivers of oil? Shall I give my firstborn for my transgression, the fruit of my body for the sin of my soul?" (vv. 6b–7). How do you calculate an offering for God's grace? In the midst of plenty, what is the measure of stewardship before the Lord? The response to this question, then as now, to a large extent defines the seriousness of our Christian faith, the depth of our spiritual quest.

Scripture has few passages that more beautifully portray the uncalculated gift of the faithful steward, the generous response of the worthy servant, than the conclusion in v. 8, "He has showed you, O man, what is good; and what does the Lord require of you but to do justice, and to love kindness [mercy, KJV], and to walk humbly with your God" (Mic. 6:8). Surrounded by prosperity, we are enjoined not to think in terms of a closely counted, respectable gift, but to respond in service to God and humankind in a spirit of justice, kindness/mercy and humility. Generosity in proportion to ability should be the key to our response, rather than a prescribed table of calculation or some customary practice. What does the Lord require in response to God's acts and God's gifts in creation? The requirement is to accept redemptive tasks at the point of our strengths, to answer the call to stewardship not out of obligation or custom but out of thanksgiving and generosity toward the challenge of the need. The strong and privileged nations and people of the world are called to steward their wealth, in a spirit of humility, as the way to do justice, kindness/mercy and peace. They will then be participating in the continuing creation process after the model of the all-giving God we have known as Creator, given and all-giving Son and gift-bearing Spirit.

The leadership ranks of churches must be composed of people whose strengths are generously committed to the challenges of the age. Devout professions of belief and pious practices by people who benefit from prosperity but do not share it are self-deceiving and religiously empty. A pastor I know recently told me of a leader in the congregation, the president-elect, who had for months opposed every proposal for mission and benevolent causes that came before the church council. Perplexed over this behavior on the part of an otherwise congenial and sincere lay person, the pastor discovered that the successful business leader and his spouse contributed less than fifty dollars per year to the congregation. It is discomforting but necessary for all people of means to understand that until our religious pursuit significantly involves the place of our treasure and our heart, the venture means nothing. The gospel claims us where we are gifted, where our heart is found.

A good steward or caretaker keeps accounts and records because management and accountability are part of stewardship. While the faith of Israel is profoundly this-worldly and both the Old and New Testaments speak in general terms about economics and worldly goods, there are few clear standards and guidelines about what the Lord requires of a person and what constitutes a worthy gift. The gift prescribed most often, particularly in the Old Testament, is the tithe. In Gen. 28:22b, for example, we hear the promise of Jacob: "And of all that thou givest me, I will give the tenth to thee." The tithe requirement includes crops, animals and a tenth of the "first fruits," all of which were to be offered in thanksgiving to God, the source of all gifts. Leviticus 27:30 says, "All the tithe of the land, whether of the seed or of the land or of the fruit of the trees, is the Lord's; it is holy to the Lord."

Two examples supporting the worthiness of the tithe as an offering in celebration of God's gifts are found in Deuteronomy 14 and 26. The general theme of Deuteronomy is a call to Israel's remembrance and faithfulness to God who has richly gifted them as a chosen people in a promised land. These chapters are a part of the section of Deuteronomy which presents the social and religious laws which are to be kept in response to God's grace, including the tithes of all first fruits given as an act of worship.

The tithe as a biblical standard of giving was not rejected

in either the New Testament or the early church, and even today is often viewed as a virtuous standard of giving. Some churches propose the half-tithe, 5 percent, as a norm that is achievable and practical for most American believers. Even this is a difficult challenge for church people who are accustomed to contributing in the range of 1 to 3 percent of their income. We laud those who give a tithe of income to church and charity. But the larger issue remains—stewarding the remaining 90 percent.

The New Testament is more in agreement with the spirit of Micah—that the Lord is worthily served not by a rigid standard or fixed amount but by a free and generous spirit with open-ended possibilities for giving. Again, Jesus serves as an example of the generous spirit of giving, not in regard to money and goods, but in the area of personal human relations and the offering of forgiveness to an offender. In Matt. 18:22, the legalistic Peter again wanted a fixed standard for forgiveness and suggested forgiving seven times one who would sin against him. Jesus, however, responded with not seven times "but seventy times seven." Do not count the cost, but act with justice, love and kindness/mercy, and walk in humility in response to need.

The same principle must apply to generosity in giving worldly goods in response to the need and in proportion to the ability of the giver. The apostle Paul, in the same spirit, suggested proportionate giving as a guideline. To the Corinthian church he wrote, "On the first day of every week, each of you is to put something aside and store it up, as he may prosper" (1 Cor. 16:2). Writing of the liberality of the Macedonian Christians who, despite their own poverty, "gave according to their means, as I can testify, and beyond their means, of their own free will" (2 Cor. 8:3), Paul urged the Corinthians to respond with gifts after the same manner.

CURRENT PRACTICES OF GIVING

After working with many congregations and leaders over a period of years, I have learned that various spoken and unspoken standards of giving are practiced. Per capita giving has long been in vogue. This is a matter of taking a budget or other specified need and dividing into it the number of supporters who are counted. The result is a per person contribution which is the same for every individual. Except for financial analysis and reporting and for painting broad financial generalizations, a per capita guideline is a low and inadequate guideline for giving. Worse, it is impersonal and artificial, wrongly assuming equal participation and ability among church members. It is far removed from the principle of giving in proportion to one's ability and one's blessings.

An even more unworthy standard of giving is what might be called "commitment by comparison" or "commitment by embarrassment." Some congregations still follow the practice of publishing quarterly the exact amounts contributed by each member or family. This tactic is often used to embarrass a member into giving at least a face-saving offering in order to maintain some respectability. It is, moreover, a kind of game members of a congregation may play: observe how others are doing and then fall somewhere within the pattern, giving not too much as to appear showy, just enough to be about average. Congregations themselves sometimes play a similar kind of cat-and-mouse game. For example, a stewardship visitor praised a congregation for its record of mission support and pointed out that the congregation, in comparison with others, ranked near the top in support of mission and outreach. Following the visit, a church leader asked the pastor why their congregation should give so generously in comparison to others, arguing that it was enough if they were somewhere "in the middle of the pack." The leader did not want his congregation to be in the forefront of generosity and liberal in support.

We often hear about fairness in giving, that it is "not fair" that one church or one person should be expected to give more generously than another. Instead of being thankful for our ability to give generously, we begrudge it. Some people and some churches are more mature and committed than others, a condition to be celebrated and not bemoaned. We must pray for those whose generosity is suppressed and nonexistent—even if we must then pray for ourselves. And we must remember that these designs and tactics that organizations and leaders employ to stimulate giving are often used to avoid generosity.

PROPORTIONATE GIVING

Many leaders have returned to the conviction that the only worthy standard of financial support for the mature Christian is proportionate, or percentage, giving, that as we have received and acquired, we give a proportionate amount. This may be a tithe or may exceed a tithe. In stewardship accountability, one will, perhaps, contribute a liberal percentage of their treasure, be it a modest or a large treasure. Many conferences of the United Church of Christ now emphasize percentage mission giving for congregations, that is, contributing to mission outreach or benevolences an amount equal to 25 percent of the total local expenditures of the congregation. One-fourth of what the congregation budgets or spends locally should be budgeted and contributed to wider mission. Since most congregations in the UCC are well below the 25 percent standard, they are encouraged to strive for the goal by annual percentage point increases.

Few and far between are the commendable congregations who are committed to giving one dollar to wider mission for every dollar spent for local ministries at home. The criterion should be that as we have been blessed and as we are truly able, so will we contribute with generous and thankful hearts. The principle affirms the belief that everything we possess and accumulate in this life is on loan to us, to be returned in full at life's end. Everything belongs to the Creator, God the Giver, for "the earth is the Lord's and the fullness thereof" (Ps. 24:1). Those of us who have received such abundance in a land of plenty are constrained to respond after the image of the Giver, to participate in the ongoing creation and to give while there is still time with thankful and generous hearts.

With our knowledge of God's endless gifts to us, what is required of us as an appropriate response? It seems clear that no legalistic schedule or sublime guideline is sufficient for our answer. Human beings in God's creation were intended to be stewards of whatever gifts came into their reach; they are not to be hoarders and misers, but free and open contributors, generous givers and employers of gifts in behalf of all unfinished creation. Following the spirit of Micah's response to the question, "With what shall I come before the Lord?" the steward's response is not calculated in cubits nor counted in careful measures. It is a full-blown, extravagant contribution, all-out, equivalent and appropriate to the need. Assessing our abundance and our strength with humility, we respond to the needs of justice with all of our gifts; we identify targets for kindness/mercy by deploying our gifts in their behalf; we seek the things that make for peace and reinforce them with our plenteous and varied gifts in every way.

Challenging the typical use of gifts are words from Dietrich Bonhoeffer:

> Earthly goods are given to be used, not collected. In the wilderness God gave Israel the manna every day, and they had

115

> no need to worry about food and drink. Indeed, if they kept any of the manna over until the next day, it went bad. In the same way the disciple must receive his portion from God every day. If he stores it up as a permanent possession, he spoils not only the gift, but himself as well, for he sets his heart on his accumulated wealth, and makes it a barrier between himself and God. Where our treasure is, there is our trust, our security, our consolation and God. Hoarding is idolatry.[2]

However, in a world that is overwhelmed by injustice, oppression and inhumanity, one comes to the question, What is the use of giving without counting the cost? Even if I were to give myself as the saints do, give toward complete emptiness and total abandonment, what difference would it make in the face of life's travail? My gift, however generous, may be wasted, squandered, pitched into a black hole and have no meaning or significance. This argument is but another excuse to retain and withhold, another reason to count the cost. In *A Track to the Water's Edge*, a sensitive compilation of the writings of Olive Schreiner, Howard Thurman shares a portion "From Three Dreams in a Desert":

> And she stood far off on the bank of the river. And she said, "For what do I go to this far land which no one has ever reached? Oh, I am alone! I am utterly alone!"
>
> And Reason, that old man, said to her, "Silence! What do you hear?"
>
> And she listened intently, And she said, "I hear a sound of feet, a thousand times ten thousand and thousands of thousands, and they beat this way!"
>
> He said, "They are the feet of those that shall follow you. Lead on! Make a track to the water's edge! Where you stand now, the ground will be beaten flat by ten thousand times ten thousand feet." And he said, "Have you seen the locusts, how they cross a stream? First one comes down to the water's edge, and it is swept away, and then another comes and then another, and then another, and at last, with their bodies piled up, a bridge is built and the rest pass over."
>
> She said, "And of those that come first, some are swept away

and heard of no more; their bodies do not even build the bridge?"

"And are swept away and are heard of no more—what of that?" he said.

"And what of that—" she said.

"They make a track to the water's edge."

"They make a track to the water's edge—" And she said, "Over that bridge which shall be built with our bodies, who will pass?"

He said, "The entire human race."

And the woman grasped her staff.

And I saw her turn down that dark path to the river.[3]

After Jesus' astounding encounter with the rich young man and his declaration about the difficulty the rich will have in entering the kingdom of God, those who heard him asked, "Then who can be saved?" (Luke 18:26). This is surely the key question of our time for Christians of the First World. Who, indeed! The rich man counted the cost of giving up his possessions and following Jesus and, deciding against it, went away sorrowful. Most Americans will probably turn away sorrowfully and stand under judgment.

Then who can be saved? Perhaps our only hope is in Jesus' final words on this subject, haunting, enigmatic words for us to ponder: "What is impossible with men is possible with God" (Luke 18:27). What can it mean? The day of reckoning? An invitation to make "a track to the water's edge," possibly participating in the bringing of a new day when sharing by all will mean scarcity for none? Or does it anticipate another miracle of grace, yet another gift of the Eternal Giver to ransom estranged spirits from enslavement to goods and property. Come, Holy Spirit, with your gift.

NOTES

Chapter 1. *The Religion of Profits and Possessions*

1. The mainline denominations of which I speak can be identified as among the founders and members of the long-developing Consultation on Church Union (COCU). An outstanding study of mainline church decline can be found in Wade Clark Roof and William McKinney, *American Mainline Religion: Its Changing Shape and Future* (Rutgers, N.J.: Rutgers University Press, 1988).

2. Harry Golden, *For 2¢ Plain* (Cleveland, Ohio: World Publishing, 1959), p. 143.

3. See the Roman Catholic church's pastoral letter, *Economic Justice for All: Catholic Social Teaching and the U.S. Economy* (1987); and *Christian Faith and Economic Life* (New York: The United Church of Christ, 1989).

4. Douglas John Hall, in an address to the Wisconsin Conference, UCC, in June 1987, at Lawrence University, Appleton.

5. Truman B. Douglass, *The Fellowship of Prayer* (Boston: United Church Press; St. Louis: Eden Publishing House, 1969), p. 53.

6. Fulton J. Sheen, *Thinking Life Through* (New York: McGraw-Hill, 1955), p. 243.

7. Jose Luis Gonzalez-Balado and Janet N. Playfoot, eds., *My Life for the Poor* (New York: Ballantine Books, 1985), p. 46.

8. Paul Tillich, *The Eternal Now* (New York: Charles Scribner's Sons, 1963), p. 183.

9. Gabriel Marcel, *Having and Being: An Existentialist Diary* (Gloucester, Mass.: Peter Smith, 1976), p. 166.

10. Elise Maclay, "Worldly Goods," in *Green Winters* (New York: Readers Digest Press, 1977), pp. 118–19.

11. Gabriel Marcel, *Having and Being*, pp. 187–88.

Chapter 2. *The Stewarding of Our Abundance*

1. Jose Luis Gonzalez-Balado and Janet N. Playfoot, *My Life for the Poor*, p. 9.

Chapter 3. *God the Endless Giver*

1. Ian Barbour, in John Baillie, *A Diary of Readings* (New York: Charles Scribner's Sons, 1955), Day 187.

2. Paul Tillich, *The Eternal Now*, p. 183.

3. Joseph A. Sittler, *Grace Notes and Other Fragments* (Philadelphia: Fortress Press, 1981), p. 72.

4. Paul Tournier, *The Meaning of Gifts* (Richmond: John Knox Press, 1968), p. 56.

5. Ibid., pp. 61–62.

6. Joseph Sittler, *Grace Notes and Other Fragments*, pp. 72–73.

Chapter 4. *Generous Hearts and Personal Possessions*

1. Helder Camara, *A Thousand Reasons for Living* (Philadelphia: Fortress Press, 1981), p. 105.

2. James A. Pike, *What Is This Treasure?* (New York: Harper & Row, 1966), p. 22.

3. *Journal of Stewardship*, vol. 40 (New York: Commission on Stewardship, National Council of Churches of Christ in the U.S.A., 1987), pp. 32–33.

Chapter 5. *Generous Hearts and Personal Relationships*

1. Albert Einstein, *The World as I See It* (New York: Philosophical Library, 1949), p. 1.

2. Paul Tournier, *The Meaning of Gifts*, p. 48.

3. Jose Luis Gonzalez-Balado and Janet N. Playfoot, *My Life for the Poor*, p. 77.

4. Ibid., pp. 16, 17, 23.

5. United Church of Christ *Book of Worship* (New York: Office for Church Life and Leadership, 1986), p. 551.

Chapter 6. *The Sacredness of Works*

1. Dietrich Bonhoeffer, *The Cost of Discipleship* (New York: Macmillan Pub. Co., 1949), pp. 337, 338.

2. Ibid., p. 341.

3. Ibid.

4. Ibid., p. 344.

5. Hans Kung, *The Church* (New York: Doubleday & Co., 1976), pp. 495, 500–501.

6. United Church of Christ *Manual on Ministry* (New York: Office for Church Life and Leadership, 1986), p. 20.

7. Jose Luis Gonzalez-Balado and Janet N. Playfoot, *My Life for the Poor*, p. 103.

8. United Church of Christ *Book of Worship*, p. 45.

Chapter 7. *The American Church and a Model Community*

1. The figures in this limited study are drawn from the 1988 Yearbook of the United Church of Christ and from its Stewardship Council reports for financial data and church statistics. The Wisconsin Department of Revenue and the Bureau of Economic Analysis, Madison, Wisconsin, have provided the income/population data by counties and metropolitan areas. All figures are for 1987.

2. Helder Camara, *A Thousand Reasons for Living*, p. 98.

Chapter 8. *The Abuse and Use of Gifts*

1. Paul Farhi, "How Much Will Baby Boomers Inherit?" *San Francisco Examiner,* March 11, 1988.

2. Howard Thurman, *With Head and Heart* (New York: Harcourt Brace Jovanovich, 1979), p. 107.

3. Howard Thurman, *The Growing Edge* (New York: Harper & Brothers, 1956), p. 143.

4. See Roger Fisher and William Urey, *Getting to Yes* (Boston: Houghton Mifflin, 1981), a steward's handbook for the caretaking of resources and relationships.

5. Paul Tillich, *The Eternal Now,* p. 185.

6. Muriel Lester, The Fellowship of Reconciliation, Nyack, New York.

Chapter 9. *Gifts Are Not Our Own*

1. Howard Thurman, *Deep Is the Hunger* (New York: Harper & Row, 1951), pp. 94–95.

2. Howard Thurman, *Meditations of the Heart* (New York: Harper & Brothers, 1953), pp. 130–32.

Chapter 10. *Ours for the Taking*

1. Helder Camara, *A Thousand Reasons for Living,* p. 108.

2. Gordon Allport, *The Person in Psychology* (Boston: Beacon Press, 1968), pp. 152, 149, 151.

3. From an interview with James Forbes in *Sojourners* (May 1989).

4. Albert Einstein, "Of Wealth," *The World as I See It,* p. 21.

5. Norman Cousins, *Dr. Schweitzer of Lambarene* (New York: Harper & Brothers, 1960), pp. 190–91.

6. Albert Schweitzer, *Out of My Life and Thought* (New York: Henry Holt & Co., 1937), p. 280.

7. Charles R. Joy, ed., *Albert Schweitzer: An Anthology* (New York: Beacon Press; Harper & Brothers, 1946), p. 268.

8. Jose Luis Gonzalez-Balado and Janet N. Playfoot, *My Life for the Poor,* pp. 92, 35.

9. Martin Luther King, Jr., *Strength to Love* (Philadelphia: Fortress Press, 1981), pp. 87–88.

Chapter 11. *Giving without Counting*

1. G. A. Studdert-Kennedy, *The Unutterable Beauty* (London: Hodder & Stoughton Ltd).

2. Dietrich Bonhoeffer, in Paul S. McElroy, *A Source Book for Christian Worship* (Cleveland: World Pub. Co., 1968), pp. 154–55.

3. Howard Thurman, ed. *A Track to the Water's Edge: The Olive Schreiner Reader* (New York: Harper & Row, 1973), pp. 55–56.

SCRIPTURE INDEX

Old Testament

New Testament